OUR FATIMA OF LIVERPOOL

The Story of Fatima Cates,
the Victorian woman
who helped found British Islam

Hamid Mahmood and Yahya Birt

BEACON BOOKS

Advance Praise for
"Our Fatima of Liverpool"

Fatima Elizabeth Cates was an exemplar of British Islam. She played a central, yet largely forgotten role, in the establishment of the first mosque in Britain and in the leadership of this nascent Muslim community. Through their telling of her story, Mahmood and Birt render an invaluable service to Muslims in Britain and beyond, to historians (including feminist historians), and to society as a whole. Their narrative is incisive, evidential and moving, and does justice to this strong woman who lived in complicated contexts.

Dr Sariya Cheruvallil-Contractor, Associate Professor in the Sociology of Islam, Centre for Trust, Peace and Social Relations, Coventry University

In this first comprehensive account of Fatima Cates' life, Mahmood and Birt provide the reader with the essence of what we only could guess at previously: a young woman who was key in founding Britain's first mosque and who suffered much, but was unflinching in her faith and her loyalty to Quilliam and her fellow converts.

Christina Longden, author of *His Own Man – A Victorian 'Hidden' Muslim – The Life and Times of Robert 'Reschid' Stanley*

This compelling account of the life and tragic death of Fatima Elizabeth Cates moves us to consider the significant role that women played in the advent of Islam in Britain, in addition to feeling the suffering of a young Victorian working-class Liverpool woman committed to establishing her newly acquired faith in opposition to all the personal, social and economic forces that embattled her from all sides.

Prof. Ron Geaves, University of Cardiff, and author of the first biography of Abdullah Quilliam, *Islam in Victorian Britain* (2010) and *Islam and Britain: Muslim Mission in an Age of Empire* (2019).

With founding figures of British Islam such as Fatima Elizabeth Cates, the urge to write a golden narrative may be strong. Yahya Birt and Hamid Mahmood have scrupulously avoided this, offering a worthy piece of historiography based on sound primary sources and mindful interpretation.

Riordan Macnamara, Senior Lecturer, University of Versailles
Saint-Quentin/Paris Saclay

First published in the UK by Beacon Books and Media Ltd
Earl Business Centre, Dowry Street, Oldham, OL8 2PF, UK.

www.beaconbooks.net

ISBN 978-1-915025-74-6 Paperback
ISBN 978-1-915025-75-3 Hardback
ISBN 978-1-915025-76-0 Ebook

Cataloging-in-Publication record for this book is available from the British Library.

Cover design by Raees Mahmood Khan

Illustration Credits: **Front cover**, Yahya Birt, Wonder App on Stable Diffusion; **Illustrations 1–8**, Hamid Mahmood, Midjourney Bot on Discord.

Picture Credits: **Picture 1**, J.H. McGovern, *Lectures in Saracenic Architecture* (Liverpool, 1896-8), frontispiece; **Picture 2**, *Wikimedia Commons*; **Picture 3**, R. Ahmad, "The Royal Marriage", *Strand Magazine* (London), Vol. VI, Jul-Sep 1893, 447–58 (458); **Picture 4**, photograph by co-author, Hamid Mahmood, 2019; **Picture 5**, B.G. Orchard, *Liverpool's Legion of Honour* (Birkenhead, 1893), facing 484; British Military Identity Certificate, Hubert Cates, No. 838723, 1920; **Picture 6**, *The San Francisco Call*, 13 Dec 1903, 17; **Picture 7**, photo by Amirah Scarisbrick, 4 November 2022; **Picture 8**, Flyer for Commemoration of Fatima Elizabeth Cates, Liverpool, 21 Jan 2023, designed by New Beginnings, Oldham.

Contents

Foreword: An Inspiring Muslima

It is with great pleasure and some trepidation that we present to you this brief biography of Fatima Elizabeth Cates (1865–1900), one of the great founding figures of Islam in Britain, and one whose sterling contribution has been forgotten or overlooked, although thankfully awareness of Fatima is beginning to grow. We acknowledge the difficulties of working with a limited archive. Only a few printed materials record Fatima's own voice, which we collect together in the appendixes here, but the rest of the historical materials that were written by others forced us to read as carefully as we could between the lines, and sometimes against the grain of these other accounts. We recognise that inevitably the reading we offer here is an interpretation but we submit that it is based on careful research and is sober in the conclusions it draws.

In her short life and with very few means at her disposal, Fatima did as much as anyone else to help build Britain's first Muslim convert community, which also founded the country's first mosque community in 1887, so far as we are currently aware. For her integrity, bravery, steadfastness and faithfulness, and for her importance to the early history of organised Muslim religious life in Britain, Fatima deserves to be better known among contemporary Muslims. We hope her story will also inspire others to strive faithfully for God and His Prophet too, and we pray that this first biography of Fatima will serve as a means to achieve that purpose.

Hamid Mahmood, London
Yahya Birt, Bradford

9 Jumada al-Awwal 1444/3 December 2022

Illustration 1: Fatima Elizabeth Cates reading a translation of the Quran.

Illustration 2: W.H. Quilliam addresses the Birkenhead Workingmen's Temperance Association on "The great Arabian teetotaler".

1

A Fateful Meeting in Birkenhead

On a summer's evening towards the end of June 1887, Frances Elizabeth Murray, a young, independently minded woman of 22, walked purposefully to a meeting being held by the Birkenhead Workingmen's Temperance Association. Frances was a dedicated Temperance campaigner, and, despite her young age, she served as the association's secretary.

The Temperance movement sought to reduce and ultimately prohibit the consumption of alcohol. Temperance was linked to many progressive causes at the time like spreading democracy, anti-slavery, socialism and trade unionism, anti-colonialism and the promotion of women's rights. It had begun in America but had become a worldwide movement, which saw the liquor trade not only as creating human misery but as a predatory business whose profits propped up unjust forces. Devout Christian women like Frances, a baptized Anglican, were at the heart of the movement.

Liverpool was in its heyday, thriving in its status as the second port (after London) of the greatest imperial power at the time, the

British Empire, which straddled the entire globe. Half of Britain's shipping and a seventh of the entire world's passed through its docks. But, like many ports, Liverpool had its dark side, of which Birkenhead was an extension on the western side of the Mersey River. Liverpool had a bad reputation as "the most drunken, the most criminal, the most pauper oppressed, the most death-stricken town in England". It had become a central battleground for the Temperance Movement in England. Some 40–50,000 seamen came in and out of Liverpool every year. Flush with unspent backpay, they supported a large economy of pubs, beer houses and brothels around the docks.

That evening's lecture in Birkenhead was to be given by the tireless, well-known local campaigner against "the demon drink" in the North-West of England, the lawyer and journalist, William Henry Quilliam. Formerly known as the Temperance Child, Quilliam had taken the pledge to abstain from all alcohol at the age of seven, and had worked as an organiser and public speaker in the movement from his teenage years, not only in Liverpool but as far afield as Scarborough. As he mounted the stage, Frances took him in. A short, energetic man of 31 years of age, Quilliam had an intelligent, piercing gaze and an unshakeable air of confidence. His reputation as a powerful and seasoned speaker preceded him, a skill he had honed not only as a Temperance speaker but from his nine years as a defence lawyer. In 1885, he had gained national attention for his defence of two Irish Fenian dynamitards, James Gilbert Cunningham and Patrick Henehan, at the Old Bailey for a conspiracy to cause bomb outrages throughout England and Scotland.

Scanning his audience of workingmen and workingwomen, Quilliam immediately warmed to his theme, which closely followed a lecture he had given two weeks earlier at the Mount Vernon Temperance Hall on 17 June, under the auspices of the

Liverpool Temperance League, called "Fanatics and Fanaticism". For the Birkenhead audience, this same lecture had been intriguingly retitled as "The great Arabian teetotaler". Quilliam argued that the Temperance Movement was often misjudged, sneered at as reactionary puritanism, with teetotalers miscast as fanatics, when they, like many other reformist figures in history, were simply misunderstood and feared and thus opposed by the forces of reaction. The exemplars Quilliam named were ones that Frances had grown up hearing about like William Wilberforce, the MP for Hull who had spearheaded the campaign for the abolition of slavery in the British Empire, and George Stephenson, who, with his son Robert, invented the locomotive steam engine, nicknamed "the Rocket", and had built the first railway line between Manchester and Liverpool.

This was diverting but familiar ground for Frances; however, it was what Quilliam said next that made her sit up and take notice. Quilliam started by alluding to someone who occupied "a far greater page in the history of the world – in fact his position is unique." He then began to talk about Mahomet (Muhammad, may the peace and blessings of God be upon him), who he asserted was far more than an Arabian imposter, as some of the more hostile missionaries of the day would have it, who dismissed Islam as morally bankrupt and as the product of the human imagination, accusing Muhammad of bad faith and dishonesty.

He was, Quilliam said, "the last and greatest of prophets", and, in offering a moving account of Muhammad's early struggles in Mecca against fierce opposition, gave examples of the privations and torture that the Prophet and followers faced from the pagan Quraysh. We know from Frances' own account of her conversion that Quilliam was challenging her own preconception that the Prophet was "an imposter and a blood-thirsty man, who forced his people to believe in his religion by threatening to put them to death, if they did not do so." Yet, despite this preconception, her curiosity had been aroused.

Frances turned to the man sat next to her, whose name was James Hamilton, and remarked, "I never knew that Muhammadans were teetotalers. I should like to know more about this religion." Providentially, Mr. Hamilton, a wholesale box maker, was none other than Quilliam's first convert. He had taken the name Ali after hearing Quilliam speak on the same topic at Mount Vernon Hall. With all the enthusiasm of the new convert, Hamilton began to explain what he knew of Islam to her and begged her to speak to Quilliam after the meeting.

Frances had more questions, even though she still held a dim view of Islam. When she talked to Quilliam afterwards she asked, "Isn't it true that the Muslim prophet said that women do not have souls and will not go to Paradise?" He said it was untrue and a lie that the enemies of Islam had spread. A few days later, Quilliam lent her his copy of the Quran to study for herself, saying, "Don't believe what I say, or what anyone else says; study the matter out for yourself." Quilliam's copy of the Quran was a reprint of a translation, the 1734 translation by the British Orientalist, Anglican and lawyer George Sale, as at the time no Muslim had translated the holy book into English.

Frances decided that she would go home and would indeed read Quilliam's copy of the Quran and make up her own mind about whether Islam was true or not.

2

Frances' Humble Beginnings

Frances was born on 5 January 1865 in Birkenhead on the Wirral at 59 Henry Street. It was a small village of just over a hundred souls in 1811, when the peninsula was still largely rural. When the Laird family moved to Birkenhead in the 1820s, they later established one of the first steel shipbuilding companies in the world, around which the village became a town. By the time Frances was born, the population had grown to around 40,000.

Her father, John Murray, an Irishman, worked as a porter at the newly built and expanding Birkenhead Market; her mother, Agnes, was from Edinburgh. Frances was the fifth of six children. He died, when Frances was only five years old, of tuberculosis, or "consumption" as the Victorians called it, accompanied by a skin infection called erysipelas. Consumption was widespread in the nineteenth century: two-thirds of the urban population had tuberculosis, and a fifth of them died from it. Alongside tuberculosis, typhus, typhoid, and smallpox were mainly diseases of the urban poor, exacerbated by overcrowding, bad diet, and lack of sanitation. Untimely deaths like that of John Murray's were all too common in this era.

The 1871 Census lists no occupation for Frances' mother, the widowed Agnes. Instead, she and her six dependents relied upon her two oldest children, David, 18, who worked as a rivetter, most likely at the Laird shipyard, and William, 15, who worked as a timekeeper, someone responsible for making sure that workers clocked in and out on time, or that trains, trams or ferries departed punctually. From the 1840s onwards, ferry, rail, and tram systems were developed in Birkenhead; for example, the first tramway system in Europe was installed in the town in 1860, which ran between Woodside and Birkenhead Park. Agnes remarried in 1873 to Peter Cottam, a widower and a stonemason, with whom she had her seventh child, Clara, a half-sister who became close to Frances.

In nineteenth-century Britain, there had been no provision of compulsory education for children, and so many poor and working-class children saw their potential wasted. With her curiosity and intelligence, Frances could have been just like them, but she was fortunate to be in the very first generation of children to benefit from the Elementary Education Act of 1870, which passed into law when she was five. This Act laid down the foundations for primary education for children between the ages of 5–12 in England and Wales, and Frances was listed as a pupil (although in those days they used the term "scholar") in the 1871 Census.

As a young adult, Frances found her passions fulfilled in joining the Temperance movement, but what motivated her to take this up is a speculative matter. We have no evidence to link the death of her father from tuberculosis to alcoholism in his case, although the link between the two was common enough in urban Victorian Britain, let alone assume this was a driving factor for Frances. However, the mix of wider progressive causes to which the Temperance movement was linked, and the opportunities it gave to women to play leading roles within it would certainly have been attractive to a talented and principled young working-class woman like Frances.

Illustration 3: The young Frances in Birkenhead.

Illustration 4: After converting, Fatima faces rejection from her family.

3

Rejection at Home

Frances returned home with Quilliam's copy of the Quran, and began to study it "carefully".

Frances tells us from her own conversion account that when Agnes, her devout Christian mother, saw her studying the scripture at home, she asked her what it was. "The Mahommedan Bible", Frances replied plainly and calmly. Agnes exploded with surprise and anger, shouting, "How dare you read such a vile and wicked book? Give it to me this moment and let me burn it. I will not allow such trash to be in my house." Frances stood firm, replying, "No, I will not, how can I know whether it is a wicked book or not until I have read it." Agnes tried to take the Quran from her daughter but Frances ran to her bedroom and locked herself in, and carried on reading. Frances was continuously scolded and threatened with all sorts of punishments if she persisted in reading the Quran, but she was not deterred in the least.

Thereafter, Frances determined that she would not leave her copy of the Quran unattended and would take it with her when she went out to stop her mother from destroying it. For her uplifting of the Quran, Frances was later honoured with its elevation in her heart as "the most precious book that could be bought".

In addition to Sale's translation, Quilliam had given her some of his own unpublished writings that explained the rudiments of Islam, comparing it favourably with Christianity and to a lesser extent with Judaism in terms of both its creed and morality, and introducing her to the Quranic narrative on the lives of the major prophets Adam, Noah, Abraham, Moses, Jesus and Muhammad. He wrote about the falseness of the Christian doctrine of the Trinity, and gave a succinct account of the Prophet's life, focusing on the first 13 years of his mission in Mecca. He summarised Islam's fundamental beliefs and its teachings on charity, social conduct and ethics, and prayer. He answered Frances' question to him in Birkenhead on the status of women in Islam by saying that God made no distinction between the sexes in terms of moral responsibility. He quoted extensively from Sale's translation of the Quran that Frances was reading at home, putting verses together thematically to buttress his argument.

Frances found Quilliam's arguments and the fruits of her self-study convincing as, within a fortnight, she began to meet regularly with Quilliam and Ali Hamilton. For weeks, just the three of them would read the Quran together and discuss it and other matters. Undaunted, Frances showed great steadfastness in going unfailingly week after week despite the attempts of her family to stop her. She was kept under constant watch and sometimes locked in a room to prevent her leaving for the meetings. Her family's "surprise and indignation" at the prospect of her becoming a Muslim also led to a lot of psychological pressure. They told Frances that she was lost, and that she had no hope of salvation if she did not reaffirm the Protestantism she had been brought up with.

But Frances held firm and, in her own words, "declared ... [herself] a Moslem". Frances became Fatima. Then her trials increased, and her family began to use all the stratagems they could think of to stop Fatima from attending the meetings. They would intercept her letters to Quilliam, and she had to endure severe satire and ridicule from them.

But Fatima was not deflected: she held firm and took her stand for Islam beyond her home and into Liverpool itself.

Illustration 5: Fatima is attacked after one of the Muslim prayer meetings.

4

The First Call at Vernon Temperance Hall

Along with Quilliam and Hamilton, Fatima was one of this first trio of pioneering converts, and the first woman to propagate Islam in Liverpool and possibly England. Together, the three of them formed the Liverpool Muslim Society on 17 July 1887, which was the first Muslim convert association in Britain. Fatima was made Treasurer of the Society. "It was very hard work at first, but we went on steadily", Fatima later recalled. She "was a constant attendant, and she soon made herself felt as an earnest worker for Islam." They rented a small upstairs room at the Vernon Temperance Hall, 14 Mount Vernon Street. The room could only be accessed by a flight of stairs on a side street called Lowndes Street. Overall, the premises were in "a dilapidated state".

Years later, the entire area was knocked down to make way for the Royal Liverpool University Hospital, and nothing now remains of the rented premises where the first attested Islamic mosque community congregated, a modest rented property that sat on the western side of Mount Vernon Street between the junctions of the long-gone Fairclough Lane and Lowndes Street. The exceptions are the old northern entrance to the street, which then takes a southward line slightly to the east of the original road, while the other survival is the Sacred Heart Catholic Church, which is about 45 metres north of where the hall would have been. Bro. Quilliam and the other Good Templars of the Liverpool Temperance League, as the officers of the Temperance movement were generally known, had established the hall at the end of 1886 for the "moral and social improvement" of the local poor in a rented house. On Thursdays, it offered free lectures, singing with piano accompaniment, readings, and the first version of the slide show called "the magic lantern". On Fridays, the Band of Hope, a Temperance institution, took pledges from local young people to give up alcohol for life.

Fatima and Quilliam based their Islamic call at Vernon Hall upon what they knew, namely, their organisational experience as Temperance activists, their Christian upbringing, and the basics of Islam. So, in isolation from other Muslims, they taught themselves as best they could. But, more than this, some of the first converts remained active in the Liverpool Temperance League *after* forming the Liverpool Muslim Society, including taking part in the organisation of a Christmas dinner for the poor in 1888. Like the written pledge to abstain from alcohol that people made to join the Good Templars, the early converts admitted themselves to Islam and signed a book of allegiance with the following pledge, thereby also joining the Liverpool Muslim Society:

> We, the undersigned, hereby acknowledge our belief in the Moslem Faith and that we hold the same and none other to be the true religion and that we believe:
>
> 1. There is only one God.
> 2. That Mahommed is his prophet.
> 3. That the Koran is the inspired book and word of God.

They would meet twice a week at the hall: on Fridays, they would meet among themselves "for prayers and reading and studying the Koran" and, on Sundays, they would have public meetings. When advertised in the local press, these Sunday meetings were described as "non-sectarian" in the summer of 1887, but although they were promoted under the auspices of the League, they may have referred to Muslim gatherings. In May 1889, these Sunday events were described more overtly in the *Liverpool Mercury*:

> Persons desirous of understanding MOSLEM THEOLOGY should attend the Sunday evening services at Vernon Hall, Mount Vernon Street, commencing at seven o'clock.

These Sunday events that Fatima, Quilliam and the others put together were modelled on the Protestant Sunday Evensong in terms of form whilst their message was Islamic. They were meant to be culturally familiar, and so kept close to forms of worship and arrangements of the service recognisable to those brought up as Christians. These elements included the singing of hymns, prayers and passages from the Quran read out from the stage, and a sermon, with the congregation arranged in rows of seats. Among the Sunday sermons that Quilliam gave at Vernon Temperance Hall were elaborations of the letters that he had written to Fatima on the fundamental beliefs and teachings of Islam, which were later published as *The Faith of Islam* in July 1889.

Like Fatima, Quilliam also saw those first months at Vernon Temperance Hall as hard work, noting that "frequently we got no audience but ourselves". But they persevered, until, Fatima recalled, "another convert was made, Mr. Wardle and then Mr. Smith, and gradually others...." For several months she was the only woman convert until a couple, Mr. and Mrs. Lester, converted. In 1887, the original three were joined by another four, then in 1888, there were another five, and then only two in 1889, bringing the overall total to 14, three of whom were women. One of them was Amina Bowman, a writer, who converted to Islam from Anglicanism, and who became close to Fatima.

Yet, as word spread about this tiny community of converts, they were subjected to horrendous intimidation, insults and violence. Fatima's steadfastness in the face of this violent opposition is noted in the *Crescent* obituary of her, and is worth quoting at length:

> It is impossible to describe the manner in which these Islamic converts were derided, the insults and indignities to which they were subjected, and the personal violence that was oft-times used against them. The windows of the little hall in which they held their meetings were repeatedly broken with stones, and roughs and Christian bigots frequently entered the room and made disturbances therein; while, in the street, the Muslims were stoned and pelted with decayed vegetable matter and rotten eggs, and followed by a crowd shouting after them. On several occasions, ruffians, unworthy of the name of men, lifted up horse manure from the road and rubbed it over our late sister's face. She endured it all, despite the fact that her family was bitterly opposed to her attending the meetings, and were horrified at the thought that she should have rejected Christianity.

After two years of toil and struggle with some success in attracting over a dozen converts, the Liverpool Muslim Society was served notice to quit Vernon Hall by their bigoted landlord who declared that he "would not have it occupied by any person who did not believe in Christ crucified as the Redeemer of the World".

Fatima and the Liverpool converts were now homeless and would have to find a new home.

5

Fatima's Leadership at Brougham Terrace

O n 20 December 1889, Fatima, Quilliam and the other converts moved into their new home – 8 Brougham Terrace, a handsome terraced house built half-a-century earlier. It faced northwards on to a busy thoroughfare, the West Derby Road, that had a lot of carriage and foot traffic. Later on, a notice was affixed outside:

Notice.

"There is no God but God, and Mahomed was His Prophet."

The Church of Islam.
Divine Service on Sundays.

Morning   11 a.m.
Evening   7 p.m.

Fatima and the others worked hard for the first public event at Brougham Terrace, a Christmas dinner for 230 poor children of the neighbourhood, who were then "amused with songs, recitations and instrumental music, and thoroughly enjoyed the treat".

In the following week, the religious services restarted but with the addition of the call to prayer, which was called out aloud in Britain for the first time from a mosque. The muezzin would make the call to prayer at 7pm on Sunday evenings from the first-floor window of the mosque above the entrance, facing northwards. The call was made twice, first in Arabic and then in English, the latter part running as follows: "Allah is great, Allah is great. I bear witness there is no God, but God. I bear witness that Mohamed is the prophet of God. Come to prayers. Come to salvation. Allah is great."

It was the call to prayer that drew in curious passers-by as well as hostile and violent attention. Fatima would reflect in 1891 that although the community now had "a nice little mosque, fairly comfortably furnished, ... the mob still annoy many of us by throwing mud and stones; however, we persevere, and are still making fresh converts."

Picture 1: Interior of Brougham Terrace, showing the stage at the rear of the mosque where the Divine Services were held on Sundays. The organ can be seen on the right.

Fatima lived through the most intense period of violent persecution that this small community of converts had to endure in the first decade of its life, after which the violence became more sporadic. Some of the incidents included the following. In the spring of 1889, while the small convert community was still at Mount Vernon Street, Fatima and her husband Hubert, still a Christian himself at that point, witnessed a party of Christians storm their meeting armed with bludgeons and brickbats. James Bartholomew Jeffrey, an old friend of Quilliam's, stopped one of the ruffians from throwing half a brick at his head. Ashamed by what his fellow Christians had done, Jeffrey converted that evening. In November 1891, a mob attacked the mosque, stoning the muezzin, and fireworks, mud, rocks and bricks were thrown at the mosque. The congregation inside was beaten and injured by what was being thrown at them. Two weeks later, a Muslim funeral was disturbed when an attempt was made to push those paying their respects into the open grave. In March 1893, the mosque's window was broken by stones and later on shards of glass were laid across the prayer area. Every front window was smashed repeatedly and the congregants often had to leave the Sunday service facing a hostile crowd outside. In January 1895, the muezzin, as he was making the call to prayer, was pelted with snowballs filled with stones, which led to a deep cut to his hand. Yet through these and other violent incidents as well as a lot of harassment and hatred that went unreported, the small community continued steadfastly in its work.

In the early years at Brougham Terrace, Fatima acted as more than just the first Treasurer of England's first mosque community, a position that she held for eight years between 1887–94, submitting annual reports to the auditor. Fatima was arguably the second most important figure in the community after Quilliam in its first decade. She and Quilliam would often represent the community externally together, for instance to the Ottoman Trade Consul for Liverpool, or to the Arab cotton traders of Manchester. She lectured regularly at Brougham Terrace but only one of her lectures survives (see Appendix I).

On one occasion at least, Fatima defended Islamic teachings in the local press. In April 1891, Fatima wrote to the *Liverpool Mercury* to correct a jibe made by a correspondent, "Esperanza", about the mistreatment of wives at the "Moslem Church of Liverpool". Fatima showed growing knowledge of Islamic jurisprudence and history in arguing that property and marriage laws were more favourable to women under Islam than they were under English law. She argued that English divorce law needed further reform to shake off the remnants of the Christian idea of marriage as a sacrament to be replaced by a civil contract based on mutual consent and dissolution with due care for the interests of any offspring, based on the principles of Islam (see Appendix I).

At the heart of Fatima's work were her efforts to proselytise Islam, and she achieved remarkable success in this regard, in her active years at Brougham Terrace between 1889 and 1894. In the first year at Brougham Terrace, in 1890, the number of converts doubled from 14 to 28. In 1891, there were 15 converts, in 1892, 33, in 1893, 17, and in 1894, six. And increasingly, women converted and came to play a more important role under Fatima's leadership: four women converted in the early Vernon Temperance Hall years between 1887–9, then five in 1890, and then eight in 1891, the years for which there is a detailed breakdown.

Overall, a quarter of the converts were women in the history of the movement, 62 in total. The 243 recorded converts tended to be middle aged, predominantly working class, Liverpudlians born-and-bred, and overwhelmingly from Christian backgrounds. The median age of the women converts was 39 (and 45 for the men), so Fatima was among the youngest in converting at 22. This relatively older age meant that one in ten converts passed away during the movement's active years.

Visiting Muslims as well as Christian missionaries trying to isolate Quilliam's community from the wider Muslim Umma would often criticize what they saw as the lack of strict gender segregation, unveiled women, and the singing of hymns accompanied by an organ at Brougham Terrace. One visiting missionary from India in 1891, Dr. Henry Martin Clark, talked to two Indian lascars at Brougham Terrace (the catch-all term deployed at the time for sailors in the British merchant fleet who were of non-European origin) who thought that the behaviour of the converts was marked by "nonsensicality" (*behudgi*) and "immodesty" (*besharmi*). However, the lascars then conceded that the converts were only adhering to local mores, or "*jaisa des waisa bhes*" (when in Rome, do as the Romans do). When later challenged by Clark on this, Quilliam responded that the convert community adhered to the ethos of the Quran:

> We try to observe the spirit of the Koran. We maintain the spirit of Islam gives women very large rights, larger in some instances than are given by the law of England. We do not try to put the women into an inferior position or anything of the kind; we would be loath to do it. We regard this rule the same as we do as to veiling; we take the words of the Koran literally to mean that they should hide their ornaments, but we do not insist on their being closely veiled.

It must have been particularly heartening for Fatima when members of her own family were drawn towards Islam. The first was her husband, Hubert Henry Cates, a marine chief engineer by profession, to whom she had been engaged for three years prior to marrying him at the Anglican St. Peters Church in Liverpool on 28 February 1889. As Fatima recalled:

35

My husband was then a Christian just as prejudiced and big-oted as my mother, and their views being the same both tried to keep me from the mosque, but in vain. He seeing I was still determined to follow it up, and thinking there must be some truth in it, commenced likewise to read the Koran, then to attend the lectures, and finally, I am happy to say, he became one of the votaries of our faith.

At the beginning of 1891, Fatima's young half-sister, Clara, then 17, was living with Fatima and her husband at 2 Marmaduke Street in Liverpool, along with some Indian Muslim students who were lodging there. She too began to take an interest in Islam. As Fatima recounts:

A younger sister of mine came to reside with me. She like my-self had been brought up, indoctrinated with all the tents of the Orthodox [sic] Church of England faith. After she had been with some few weeks she expressed a desire to attend one of the public lectures that we held in the lecture hall of our Moslem Institute. The lecturer was Mr. Quilliam, and he took for his subject, "Fables of ancient times," and pointed out to the audience how all religions, except Islam, had become corrupted by the addition of silly myths and traditions, and shewed how much simpler and purer the faith of Islam was than that of other creeds.

When we got home my sister remarked how easy it was to understand and follow such a lecture, and how different it was to the dry and uninteresting theological discourses she had heard in Christian Churches, and stated she would like to hear more about Islam. The result was that in the course of about three months she also became a Moslem.

After she converted, Clara Haleema married one of the young Indian students lodging at the same residence as Fatima and her in around 1892. He was a young Bengali named Syed Abdul-Haleem, who was studying law, first in Liverpool and later in Cambridge. He also served as Honorary Secretary to the London Anjuman-i-Islam or Islamic Association, which had been set up in 1886. After marriage, Clara and Syed returned to Calcutta and settled there, where she had two children, a boy and a girl, and then a third whose gender is not known to us at the time of writing. Sadly, Syed died in 1902. Fatima's obituary notes that another one of her siblings, most likely her older sister Annie Maria (b. 1862), also converted to Islam and married an Indian barrister-at-law, Mr. Ghoosh, with whom she had a child, Enid.

Fatima promised to publish another article on "how the work of proselytising could be most successfully carried on amongst females and children in England" but this did not happen. Therefore, all that can be done is to piece together what is known about some of the other early women converts whom Fatima influenced.

One was Alice Bertha Bowman (1854–1940), the third woman to convert to Islam in Liverpool, in 1888, when the fledgling community was still based at Mount Vernon Street. She took the name "Amina". At the time, she lived in Tranmere, about a mile away from Fatima in Birkenhead, so it is reasonable to assume that Fatima was her conduit to Islam. Despite her father dying at the age of four, Alice had a happy childhood, developing a love of nature, particularly of the night sky, and she formed a close relationship with her stepfather. From her poetry and prose, her intense faith stands out, based on her personal experience of the Divine gained through contemplation of His creation. She remained a restless soul, getting baptized in the Anglican Church at 20 before converting to Islam 14 years later. Her conversion inspired a creative period on her part and an opportunity to publish her prose and poetry in the *Allahabad Review*, the main outlet for Liverpool Muslims alongside the Liverpool press before they launched their own periodicals in

37

1893. Bowman was the most prominent of the Liverpool Muslims in this Indian journal, publishing seven articles and three poems, most of which dwelt on spiritual reflection upon the self and upon nature, and were rarely explicitly Islamic in content, for example, this stanza from her poem, "Thoughts While Alone in the Country":

> The flowers surrounding me, are of a beautiful hue,
> And to only one hand, is their perfection due,
> While the green of the fields, and tinted skies of blue,
> Whisper to me of heaven, and all that's holy and true.

Alice married another Vernon Temperance Hall convert under Islamic rites, George Khalid Smith, a detective, who had become Muslim in 1887. They had a son, Frederick, in January 1894, followed by an Anglican marriage in April that same year to formalise their earlier Islamic matrimony. The switch of both husband and wife to the printing trade in the 1890s is tantalizing: were they employed by Quilliam as a trusted, senior "Vernon Hall" convert couple to run his printing business, established in 1893, which produced the weekly *Crescent* and the journal *The Islamic World* among other items? Khalid changes his profession from detective in the register of allegiance (1887) to printer (1894 marriage certificate). Amina lists herself as an authoress early on in 1888 (in the Book of Allegiance) but in the 1901 Census her profession is listed as a printer's roller composition manager.

Whatever the truth of the matter about Khalid and Amina's possible respective roles as Quilliam's printer and compositor, they both remained active members of the Liverpool Muslim community in other respects throughout the 1890s. Amina was part of the committee that ran the Medina Home for Children that was set up in 1896 and often donated to it, while Khalid Smith often deputized for Quilliam at the Sunday services and lectured in his stead when he was away as well as taking an active role in the Institute's Debating Society. Amina did not remain an active part of the community after 1900, and seems to have moved away from a strict adherence to Islam as she had her son baptized, belatedly at the age of 11, in January 1905. Frederick, her only child, later had a career as an actor and playwright and remained close to his mother, often casting her as his leading lady; his posthumous profile in the *Liverpool Echo* depicts a flamboyant, eccentric man of strong convictions, who was both a convinced pacifist and vegetarian. He died in 1969 of pneumonia and was cremated.

Another early convert whom Fatima is likely to have had a role in calling to Islam was Hannah Rodda Robinson (1854–1948). Losing her father to tuberculosis at the age of two, Hannah grew up in poverty in London's East End, spending periods in the workhouse. Later on she worked as a housemaid for Dr. Geoffrey Pearl, one of Victoria's physicians, and in 1875 had an illegitimate child with him. In 1880, Hannah married Spencer Robinson, a tea farmer from Darjeeling in India, where she settled and had several children. Spencer died in 1889 and Hannah returned to Brighton, England, where she ran an upmarket boarding house. In 1891, she met Dr. Gholab Shah, purportedly an Afghan warlord who had battled against the British in the Second Anglo-Afghan War. They were married in Liverpool by Abdullah Quilliam that year, one of the first Islamic marriages at the mosque in Brougham Terrace, which had been preceded by a civil wedding in London.

Quilliam oddly claimed at the time that it was his first wife, Hannah, a committed Wesleyan all her life, who played a role in convincing Hannah Rodda Robinson of Islam, but this seems highly unlikely. Gareth Winrow, Hannah's biographer, thinks that this role was most likely played by Fatima Cates, due to her leading role in this regard at Brougham Terrace. Hannah became Fatma, and the new couple moved to Constantinople. The marriage quickly collapsed when Shah was found to be an imposter, an Indian eye doctor named Eliahie Bosche, who married English women for their wealth. Stranded in Istanbul, Fatma wrote to the Grand Vizier and Sultan Abdul Hamid II for aid who then supported her and gave her children free education and legal support so that she could be granted a divorce. Fatma married for a final time to an Ottoman military officer, Ahmet Bahri, and she remained in Istanbul until her death. Her son, Ahmet Robinson, achieved sporting fame in Turkey by becoming Galatasaray's first goalkeeper and for introducing scouting and basketball to the country.

It is notable that in 1891, in conversation with the missionary Dr. Clark, one observer who was well acquainted with Brougham Terrace said that "there is nothing of devotion about any of them, except some of the women." This was perhaps a backhanded compliment about Fatima's leadership. In 1891, Fatima wrote a hymn, "A Moslimah's Prayer", whose opening lines eloquently sum up her courage, faith, and perseverance during these testing years:

> Beset by numerous foes,
> Concealed along the way,
> We must those enemies oppose,
> And ever work and pray.

6

Fatima and the Indian Muslims

Although it is not known exactly how it happened, the Indian Muslims first received word in 1889 of a convert community in Liverpool while it was still based at 14 Mount Vernon Street in an upstairs rented room. As the Liverpool Muslims had yet to garner international press attention, it seems most probable that the news went back to British India via Indian student or sailor networks. Those most immediately engaged by the news were the wealthy, Anglicized Indian Muslims influenced by the religious and educational reform programme exemplified by Sayyid Ahmad Khan (1817–98), who founded the Muhammadan Anglo-Oriental College in the 1870s. This class emphasized modern education for Muslims and they set up associations (*anjumans*) in cities like Allahabad, Amritsar, Bombay, Calcutta, Hyderabad, Lahore, and Madras to support these new educational projects, operating as philanthropic and social clubs. Active in these associations were young Indian Muslim men eager to study medicine, law or some other degree in Britain, and, as an extension of these associations, the London Anjuman-i-Islam was established in 1886.

One of these was Rafiuddin Ahmad (1865–1954) from Poona, who left India for England in June 1889 to study law, who, as a former Vice-President of the Bombay Anjuman-i-Islam, was appointed by them to act as their "Moslem agent in England ... to look after the political and religious interests of his community". Ahmad quickly became involved in both the London *anjuman* and in Quilliam's Liverpool Muslim Society (as the institution in Brougham Terrace was known at the time). As Quilliam and his fellow converts had effectively admitted themselves to Islam, and formed a society, Ahmad gathered them together to formally make the declaration of faith (*shahada*) when he came to Liverpool. In 1890, Ahmad was appointed the Society's Vice-President, and he had a major impact on the Liverpool Muslims in terms of how they campaigned politically on Muslim issues, pushing them to formalise their running as an organisation, and, most importantly, connecting them to the wider Islamic world, specifically to Muslims in British India and to the Ottoman caliphate, which was essential to raising their profile for networking, campaigns, and fundraising. Fatima played an important role in both re-establishing the Society as the Liverpool Muslim Institute in 1890 and in promoting the Liverpool Muslims in India from 1890 to 1893.

From the beginning of 1890, Rafiuddin used his contacts to build the Liverpool Muslims' profile among the Indian Muslim associations. In February that year, at the annual meeting of the Anjuman Himayat-i-Islam in Lahore, a delegate from Rangoon read a letter from Quilliam as the founder of "the Mohammedan Anjuman of Liverpool" asking for financial assistance, rather than for aid in proselytizing Islam. Fatima also led on this promotional campaign, as "the local secretary of the Liverpool Moslem Society"

From a Photo. by]   MOULVIE RAFIUDDIN AHMAD.   [Elliott & Fry.

*Picture 2: Rafiuddin Ahmed (1865–1954) who did much to promote
Fatima as one of the leading Liverpool converts among Indian Muslims
in the early 1890s.*

by writing to contacts in Hyderabad in the autumn of 1890, asking for financial assistance, to aid the 25 English converts in promoting their mission of "converting the English people". Plans to send Indian Muslim missionaries to Liverpool were quickly drawn up in Hyderabad under Maulana Hasan Ali of Patna and from Bareilly a Muslim guide for the Liverpool converts was prepared by Maulana Riazuddin Ahmad, but Rafiuddin Ahmad backed Quilliam's position by insisting that

> You have no need to invite preachers and missionaries from abroad, because every single member of this organisation is himself an active missionary. To fulfil the responsibilities of the noble cause that you have undertaken, all you require is some financial assistance.

Besides these fundraising efforts in British India, it was Rafiuddin Ahmad's leading role in the campaign against the proposed staging of a play, *Mahomet*, at the Lyceum in London, that helped to bring the Liverpool converts to the attention of other parts of the Muslim world. Although it was the Indian Muslims of Calcutta and Bombay who led the way with petitions, pamphleteering, public meetings and boycotts of city theatres, Ahmad published a letter in the *Times* to the Conservative Prime Minister of the day, Robert Gascoyne-Cecil, arguing that to stage the play would offend Indian Muslims and be harmful to Britain's imperial interests. Significantly, he signed the letter as "Vice-President of the Liverpool Moslem Association".

By this time, the Liverpool Muslims had begun to attract the attention of the Ottomans, and its local trade consul in Liverpool was asked to report back on them to the London embassy. Ahmad then wrote to Sultan Abdul Hamid II via the London embassy, introducing himself as vice-president and the converts who made up the "Moslem Association of Liverpool" but without mentioning the president, Quilliam, at all. Two months later a reply was sent, but not to Ahmad: rather, it was Quilliam who received a response from the English aide-de-camp general to the Sultan, Vice Admiral Woods Pasha. This led to Quilliam's first visit to Istanbul in 1891 and, eventually, to the development of a closer relationship with the Ottomans, who came to eclipse the Indian Muslims as Quilliam's favoured patrons, although the latter remitted significant amounts in 1892 to pay for equity in 11 and 12 Brougham Terrace and for a printing press, from which the Institute's periodicals would be produced from 1893 onwards.

It seems that this Ottoman rebuffled to some distancing between Quilliam and Ahmad, who left his position as Vice-President in 1891, although, two years later, Ahmad was able to get an introduction to the Ottoman caliph as Queen Victoria's self-styled representative through his friendship with her Urdu teacher and personal servant, Munshi Abdul Karim. This led to him being vilified as a dangerous pan-Islamist by the Foreign Office and Victoria's courtiers, who did not like the influence or access to sensitive information that he might have had through Abdul Karim. In truth, Ahmad was always more of an "empire loyalist", albeit one who worked assiduously for Muslim empowerment. In later life, he was knighted by the British for his distinguished legal career in British India.

But if Quilliam's ties with Indian Muslims took on more of a secondary role, this was not the case with Fatima. Indeed, if anything, her ties with the Indian Muslims strengthened rather than weakened. Alongside her fellow Liverpudlian convert, Amina Bowman, Fatima became the trusted face of the Society, now rebooted as the Liverpool Muslim Institute (LMI) to the Indian Muslims. In 1890, the names of the officers of the Institute, listing F.E. Cates as Treasurer, alongside its Constitution and General Rules, were publicized among the Indian Muslim associations; thus far, two notices have been uncovered for that year from the *anjuman*s in Lahore and Allahabad.

*Picture 3: The Begum of Bhopal, Shahjehan Begum Sahiba
(r. 1868–1901), about whom Fatima wrote a poem in 1893.*

Between 1891 and 1893, after Ahmad had left his position as Vice-President, the *Allahabad Review* published three essential pieces by Fatima, which all feature in Appendix I. The first, "How I Became a Mahommedan", was Fatima's personal account of converting to Islam and the trials she endured thereafter as one of the early converts, both at home and in wider society. The second was her poem and hymn, "A Moslimah's Prayer", which trenchantly echoes her early struggles mixed with her fervent prayers for Heaven. The third, "The Liverpool Converts: Correct Details", demonstrates that Fatima was trusted among the Indian Muslims as a competent and scrupulous officer of the Institute. The list is of great historical value as it preserves the names and details of the first 41 adult converts in their original sequence of conversion from the actual register, or the "Book of Allegiance" as it was called, kept by the Liverpool Muslim Society then by Liverpool Muslim Institute in the first five years of the community's life.

Fatima's final piece is a poem, "Khadija", which demonstrates her growing knowledge of and attachment towards Indian Muslims. It was written in praise of the Begum of Bhopal, Shahjehan Begum Sahiba (r. 1868–1901), the third of four female rulers of a major princely state in British India, founded by Dost Mohammad Khan with the ending of the Mughal Empire. Shahjehan was known for her patronage of the arts and architecture. She also composed poetry and prose, writing as "Tajwar" for her Urdu works and as "Shirin" for her Persian works. Most pertinently, Shahjehan paid special regard to Muslims in Britain. She contributed two-thirds of the costs (£10,000) towards the building of the first purpose-built mosque in England, commissioned by G.W. Leitner (1840–99), the Hungarian Orientalist and educationist. A pretty Mughal miniature, it was completed in August 1889, and Leitner stipulated that it serve solely as a campus prayer facility for the private use of his students at the Oriental College in Woking, Surrey (it only opened as a mosque, as a public place of prayer, much later in 1913), for which he was publicly criticized by Quilliam and others.

Fatima's poem praises Shahjehan for her virtues of righteousness, mercy, truth and equity and prays earnestly for her share of Heaven. The meaning of the reference to "Khadija" in the poem's title is open to interpretation: perhaps Fatima saw Shahjehan as an inspiring example of Muslima leadership for British Muslims, one who supported Islam in Britain at its foundations by being the first to give it aid and comfort when no one else had, just as Khadija did for the Prophet after the first revelation. Perhaps Fatima also hoped too that the cause of Liverpool would come to the Begum's attention just as Woking's had.

Beyond the hurly-burly of representing the Liverpool Muslim Institute on the international stage, Fatima's connections to Indian Muslims became very personal. When Fatima, her husband, Hubert Henry, and her half-sister Clara lived together at 2 Marmaduke Street, they took in two Indian Muslim law students as lodgers. One of them was Syed Abdul Haleem, who was a member of the Liverpool Muslim Institute and who also served for a time as the Honorary Secretary of the London Anjuman-i-Islam. He married Clara Haleema in around 1892, and had three children with her. As mentioned previously, another sister of Fatima's, Annie, had married the Indian barrister, Mr. Ghoosh. It is not too hard to imagine that later on the two sisters, Fatima and Clara, kept in touch about family life by correspondence, sending letters between Liverpool and Calcutta, after Clara had emigrated there.

7

A Violent, Murderous Husband

It might be imagined that Fatima found respite and comfort in her husband during the trials she had undergone to uphold the way of Islam. After all, despite his initial hostility and scepticism, Hubert Henry Cates had embraced the faith at Brougham Terrace in 1890, three years after she had, and had become Haleem. Indeed, that might be how it seemed to most in the small community of converts at Brougham Terrace, but the reality behind closed doors in Fatima's home was far from supportive. These revelations are based upon the Divorce Petition that Fatima lodged against her husband in 1891, which is included in Appendix II. Due to the penchant for euphemism found in Victorian legal documents, the language used there tends to understate and not convey the full trauma of what Fatima suffered at the hands of her husband.

Hubert's work as a chief marine engineer meant that he was often away at sea. But, if there was a honeymoon period, it did not last long. Four months after they were married, Cates flew into a rage when everyone else was out and smashed several pictures hanging on the wall with a pair of brass fire tongs. He threatened to smash Fatima's head in with them, at which she fainted and remained unconscious for several hours. Such was Hubert's instability that he twice threatened to commit suicide by taking poison to emotionally blackmail Fatima and to cow her into submission.

Nearly a year later, in March 1890, there came the first physical assault. Cates beat Fatima and abused her, and struck her savagely twice on the head. Cates then locked her in a room and threatened to hurt her again. Fatima managed to escape and sought refuge at the home of "a mutual friend", possibly Quilliam. The couple agreed to a separation on 24 March and Fatima and Cates decided to live apart. The Divorce Petition states that, at the time, Cates was having affairs with two women, one named Maggie Butler and another who was only known by her first name, Alice.

Sometime later, Fatima agreed to give her husband another chance after he had made "many promises of amendment and future good behaviour and expressing great contrition for his past conduct". For a trial period of six months, they were to share a roof but not a bedroom. It was during 1890 that Fatima addressed the convert community "On the Folly of Heeding Scandal", the only one of her lectures to survive (see Appendix I). While her talk was of general moral import, there might have been a personal motive at play here if tongues had started to wag at the mosque about the state of the Cates' marriage. Subsequently, Fatima thought it prudent not to be alone with Cates, so they moved to a larger residence at 2 Marmaduke Street. There, Fatima had her sister Clara staying with her, as well as taking in two lodgers, the Indian law students, Syed Abdul Haleem and Ahmad Mohammed.

However, despite these precautions, in February 1891, Cates beat Fatima again. He locked Fatima and himself into her bedroom. He seized both her wrists and forced her down to the ground, bruising her arms terribly. He threatened to hurt her and said he would kill her. In desperation, to attract the attention and help of Clara and the others, Fatima broke several panes of glass in the window. In doing so, she cut her hands severely. On another occasion in Marmaduke Street, Cates came into her bedroom and, holding a knife to her throat, threatened to slash her neck. It was only with great difficulty that Fatima escaped her murderous husband.

Picture 4: 2 Marmaduke Street, Liverpool (centre), where Fatima faced severe domestic violence from her husband.

It was a few months later that Fatima wrote to the *Liverpool Mercury* on "The Marriage Question" to advocate for the reform of English divorce law to allow for separation on the basis of mutual consent. She had seen the shortcomings of the current divorce law from bitter personal experience, which, under the Matrimonial Causes Act of 1857, only allowed women to file for divorce on the grounds of "incest, bigamy, and adultery with cruelty or four years' desertion." She well understood that it was an unjust law, which meant that divorce was essentially in the hands of husbands. Along with the Muslim lawyers, W.H. Abdullah Quilliam and Rafiuddin Ahmad, whom she knew well and whose writings she had studied, Fatima reasoned that the Islamic view of marriage as contractual rather than sacramental showed the way forward to reform English divorce law.

Unashamed, Cates now began to insult Fatima in public places, shouting at her, insulting her, using foul language and telling her to go to Hell. It was at this time, in September 1891, that Fatima wrote her great hymn and poem, "A Moslimah's Prayer" (see Appendix I). As it is highly autobiographical, is it possible that the poem's second stanza is a veiled reference not only to those who assailed the Liverpool Muslims simply for their faith, both inside and outside the mosque, but also to Cates, who was also one of the "ravening beasts of prey" who "watched but to devour" his wife?

Finally, on 7 December 1891, Cates assaulted Fatima again. He struck a violent blow on her head, causing blood to flow from her ear. Cates then picked up a heavy iron poker and threatened to "brain" her. He raised the iron above his head and made to strike her, but, by God's mercy, Clara stopped him from murdering Fatima. The sisters immediately went and laid charges against Cates at the Petty Sessional Court.

Two days later, at the Police Courts in Dale Street, Cates was charged and pleaded guilty to aggravated assault. A court order was made for judicial separation and Cates was fined £20 to keep the peace for a period of 12 months. Notwithstanding the court order to keep the peace, Cates continued to make threats of violence to Fatima, and so she had to resort to police protection.

For all practicable intents and purposes, their violent and abusive marriage was at an end, but while they most likely remained estranged after 1891, Fatima's petition for divorce was never granted, and she was only given a judicial separation.

8

Travel to the East

It was not often that Fatima managed to get some respite from the trials and cares of her life, but as a Muslima who read the Quran translation of George Sale attentively, Fatima will have read the fifth verse from the ninety-fourth chapter that runs, "Verily a difficulty shall be attended with ease."

And so it was that she was granted some ease, an opportunity to travel to the lands of Islam with two fellow English Muslimas. In October 1892, Fatima boarded the S.S. Anubis with Mrs. Amy Amina Mokaiesh and Miss Leah Zuleika Banks to visit "various Eastern Moslem cities". In a journey that took a few weeks, the S.S. Anubis stopped at Gibraltar, Malta, Alexandria in Egypt, and Larnaca in Cyprus. Fatima and her friends stayed out in the Middle East for several months before returning in May 1893. We don't know precisely where the three English Muslimas went but we may make some educated guesses by looking more into the connections Fatima and her friends had.

Born in 1864 in Scarborough on the Yorkshire coast, Leah Banks was the fifth youngest of six daughters, and came from a Wesleyan family. Her father was a ship rigger. From her teenage years onwards, Leah worked as a live-in domestic servant to the Hawson family of Falsgrave, a small town west of Scarborough. At some point thereafter, Leah moved to work as a domestic servant and cook for the Ratcliffe family of Birkenhead, Cheshire. Leah is listed as living with the Ratcliffes in the 1891 Census, so we can assume that Leah had somehow come into contact with Fatima Cates, who kept in regular touch with her own family who also lived in Birkenhead. In 1891, Leah embraced Islam and joined the Liverpool Muslim Institute, signing her name in the Book of Allegiance, and took the name Zuleika. She married another Muslim convert W.G. Ismail Winter (1849–1904) at the mosque, who was a plumber and painter by trade, and who served for a time as an LMI committee member. Their two children, Dorothy (b.1894) and Frederick (b.1896) continued to attend the mosque after their father's death. Leah Zuleika later took up self-employment as a dressmaker to support her children. From the little that we know about her, it does not appear that she had previous connections in the Middle East, but that was not the case with Fatima.

Prior to her trip, Fatima had travelled with Quilliam to Manchester earlier in 1892 on LMI business where they met some Egyptian Muslim traders, one of whom, "A.H.", later wrote about the meeting in a Cairo journal, *Al-Ustadh*. So it might well be that if Fatima spent time in Egypt on this journey, then she had some prior connections she could have used.

Fatima's other travel companion was Amy Amina Mokaiesh (b.1865) who was born Amy Ogden into an Anglican family from Rusholme, Lancashire, the fifth youngest of six children. Amy's father was a paper merchant, a manager at the Bombay Paper Mills in Manchester. Sometime in her early twenties, Amy met Ali Mokaiesh (Muhayyish, b. 1856), a Syrian cotton trader from a wealthy Beirut family. He had come to Manchester in 1884 to launch the family

Illustration 6: Fatima imagined at the Great Mosque of Damascus in 1893. It is likely her journey to the Middle East for several months did take her to Beirut, so it is possible that she went on from there to Damascus.

textile business there. They married under Islamic law and had a child, Freda, in 1890, and lived in Didsbury, Chorlton-cum-Hardy, like other Levantine merchants did at the time. Amy was his second wife (the first was in Beirut). Although the one report we have only names the three women travelling together, it may have been the case that Amy was also travelling with her husband and two-year-old daughter to meet her in-laws in Beirut. Given Amina's family connections it seems likely that the whole party did go to Beirut from Larnaca (under 130 miles by ship) and then possibly on to Damascus as part of their extended stay in the Middle East.

Later on, Ali had a civil marriage with Amina in 1895. Like the other Syrian Ottoman traders in Manchester, Mokaiesh played an active role in the LMI after its recognition by the Ottomans in 1890, and would travel to Liverpool to attend Eid celebrations, the mawlid, or celebrations of the Sultan's birthday, or attending upon Ottoman officials who were passing through Liverpool and were visiting the mosque. Sometimes Mokaiesh would officiate as an imam at the Institute. Ali's business did not fare well, however, and he became bankrupt in 1896. He absconded with Amina and Freda to Beirut to avoid his creditors; Quilliam would defend his case. Later, they moved to Cairo, and Freda had a career as a famous singer.

Besides this long trip to the Middle East in 1892–3, Fatima went on another trip to the South of England "for a considerable period" in 1895 where she spent time photographing the landscape; later on, her photobook of this trip, "one large volume of photographs of scenery", was donated to the Institute's library. The year 1894 was Fatima's last as Treasurer, and, although *The Crescent* had begun publication the previous year, Fatima's name appears infrequently in its editorial notes, which meticulously record the social and religious affairs of the mosque community. Notwithstanding the fact that *The Crescent*'s issues for 1894 are lost, it can be assumed that William Abdur-Rahman Holehouse, Quilliam's stepfather, took over the role of Treasurer that year because he was re-elected to the position at the Institute's Annual General Meeting in August 1895. At that same AGM, Fatima was re-elected in her absence to the Ladies Committee, presided over by Quilliam's mother, Harriet Khadijah Quilliam-Holehouse (1832–1901), who had converted in 1893. It can therefore be assumed that Fatima's level of active involvement in the life of the Institute began to wane after 1894.

Illustration 7: Fatima with Hubert Haleem at her home in West Kirby in the late 1890s.

9

A Lonely Widow

On 7 November 1900, *The Crescent* dolefully published the following stark news:

> It is our melancholy duty to announce the somewhat sudden demise of one who took a very prominent position in the early propaganda of the Islamic cause in England, namely, our Sister Fatima Elizabeth Cates.

After recounting her great effort and struggles for the early community in the late 1880s and early 1890s, *The Crescent* continued:

> Up to the time of his death, which occurred in the month of January, 1896, Bro. Cates always attended the services at the Mosque throughout the periods he was on shore, and he read several papers before the Literary and Debating Society, his wife taking a deep interest in the work. The union was only blessed with one child, a boy, who was born about five months after his father's death, and who is now, therefore, left parentless. After her husband's death Mrs. Cates removed to West Kirby, where she supported herself and her son by keeping a boarding house and letting furnished apartments. For the last

two years she did not enjoy good health, and in consequence of the distance she lived out of town, and the necessity of attending to her household duties, she did not visit the Mosque regularly, but her interest in the same never flagged, and she painted a very beautiful vase, ornamenting it with flowers and a text from the Koran, and presented it to the Institution. This gift stands at present on the platform in the lecture hall.

This narrative of the lonely widow grieved over the loss of a dutiful husband was written in *The Crescent* by "H. Mustafa Léon", portrayed as a doctor and a French convert to Islam who played an active role in the last decade of the Institute's life. But it was in fact a *nom de plume* that Quilliam used to talk about himself and others in the third person. "Léon" continues in the third person to explain Fatima's rapid decline in health and her faithful demise:

> Some ten days prior to her demise she contracted a severe cold, and on Wednesday, October 24, was too ill to leave her bedroom. At the time it was not contemplated anything was seriously the matter with her beyond an attack of influenza. On Saturday, the 27th ultimo, she was very much worse, and medical aid was called in, but next day she appeared to be much better. On the Monday morning [29 October 1900], however, acute pneumonia supervened, and at three o'clock the doctor pronounced that there was no hope. Telephonic message was at once sent to the Sheikh-ul-Islam [Abdullah Quilliam], who proceeded to the house. Sister Cates was perfectly conscious, and expressed to him her wish to be buried as a Muslim, as she would die in the Faith she had embraced, and further desired him to conduct the funeral service over her grave, and to be guardian to her little boy. Half an hour later she expired.
>
> A few moments before she died our sister raised the index finger of her right hand, and slowly, but clearly, repeated the *Kaleema* in Arabic, then putting her hand in that of the Sheikh, she smiled a sweet smile and said, "Goodbye; it is all over," and without a struggle peacefully yielded up her breath.

10

A Moving Funeral

Two days later, on Wednesday 31 October 1900, Fatima Cates, the woman who helped to found British Islam was buried at Anfield Cemetery. She was the first Muslim to be buried there, and, as such, her funeral attracted the attention of Christians who came to observe their first Muslim funeral. It was a small but heartfelt affair as Fatima was held in high regard by those who knew her. The grief expressed was spontaneous, and "conventionalities were conspicuous by their absence." Leaving aside ostentation, for the service:

> Everything was simple, quiet but beautifully imposing and impressive, and the tout ensemble acted upon non-Muslims as had nothing previously in their recollection. The obsequies were performed just within the Mosque portals and at the graveside in Arabic and English by the Sheikh (Abdullah Quilliam Effendi), and the prayers offered before the committal service were repeated by a company of little fellows from the Medina Home [the orphanage set up by the LMI in 1896].

The chief mourners listed in *The Crescent* included Fatima's closest family and friends. Her mother, Agnes Murray, Fatima's young son, Hubert, and all her sisters – Sarah Murray Duckett with her husband, Charles, Mary Ellen "Polly" Murray, Agnes "Aggie" Murray, and Annie-Maria Murray-Ghoosh with her daughter, Enid – save for Clara who was in India with her family. Two of her oldest Muslima friends were there too, Bertha Amina Smith née Bowman, Leah Zuleika Winter née Banks with her husband, Ismail Winter, and Prof. Henry Nasrullah Warren (1866–1930), who had converted in 1890.

The official *Crescent* account of Fatima's funeral by George Henry Green emphasized Quilliam's closeness to Fatima, in his role as the religious leader of the Muslim community in Liverpool:

> The Sheikh was in attendance in what may be coldly described as his official capacity. He was also there as the man who received the deceased lady into the faith, who throughout his valiant struggle for Islam was ever loyally aided by the woman whose soul had returned to its maker, and who grasped the kind hand and comforted the pure and holy mind of the beloved creature in the awful moments of transition. Mrs. Cates' husband was one of the warmest friends of the Sheikh, who watched the career of her child with all the affection and pride of a loving guardian.
>
> [...] The inspiring, pathetic, yet hopeful recitation by the tomb held the group spellbound, and as the Sheikh plaintively uttered the closing syllables his voice became almost inaudible, and the atmosphere was filled with a reverent solemnity that overcame the sensations. The Sheikh gazed down on the thin, plain coffin which encased the remains of a pious woman, a true wife, an adoring mother – remains of a woman who had fulfilled, if ever one did, God's mission on Earth; the tiny, parentless boy stood awed by the brink of the grave; the fond and aged mother sobbed and trembled as the daughter's corpse disappeared – there were a few dry eyes, but only a few.

Illustration 8: Fatima's funeral at Anfield Cemetery in 1900.

As the Sheikh cast dust upon Fatima's coffin, and the grave was about be filled, he addressed her directly in a loud voice:

> O Fatima, say at the Gate of Heaven, and on the Day of Examination, there is only one God, and Mahomet is His Prophet! Oh, thou soul, which art at rest, return unto thy Lord, well pleased with thy reward and well pleasing unto God.

And thus ended the authorized account of Fatima's later life and death.

11

The Secret Third Wife

The lonely widow narrative that *The Crescent* gave after Fatima's death begins to crumble when we go back through earlier issues of *The Crescent* itself. In Fatima's obituary from 1900, Cates' death was given as January 1896, with his son, Hubert, born posthumously five months later. However, despite the fact that this weekly magazine made a habit of noting the deaths of its members and sometimes publishing obituaries of them, there is nothing to be found on Cates in Vol. VII for 1896. Instead, *The Crescent* records Cates' sudden death at sea on 2 January 1895, a full year earlier, and Quilliam even penned a poem to mark his passing:

> Oh! silent hearts, for ever passed
> > Beyond the reach of strife and care,
> Lie calmly still in dreamless sleep,
> > Nor know the grief we have to share.
>
> While your freed spirits upward fly
> > On wings of love from sphere to sphere,
> Until before Great Allah's throne
> > You stand, and, trusting, answer, "Here!"

Yet, Fatima's son was born, as his official birth certificate declares, on 19 May 1896, seventeen months later. Thus, the father could not have been Cates. Rather, the circumstantial evidence points strongly towards Quilliam himself being the father.

The first piece of evidence is the name on the birth certificate: Hubert Haleem Quilliam Cates. The second piece of evidence is Hubert Haleem's birthplace on his birth certificate, which was 30 Elizabeth Street, right next door to Quilliam's Crescent Printing Works at 32; this is relevant as Quilliam inherited a lot of properties in Liverpool through his paternal grandfather, bought from the proceeds of his watch manufacturing companies and his land speculations. The third is the cover-up itself, which was orchestrated by Quilliam as the editor-in-chief of *The Crescent*. However, a careful examination of the official "lonely widow" narrative in the Institute's weekly newspaper turns up hints of a much closer relationship. Half-an-hour before her demise, Quilliam is granted guardianship of Hubert Haleem. Fatima dies with Quilliam at her side: she held his hand, while he comforted her. Her obituarist, George Henry Green, describes Fatima as a "beloved creature", the context being her last moments with Quilliam. He watches the career of Hubert Haleem from birth "with all the affection and pride of a loving guardian". At the funeral, leading the prayers for Fatima, Quilliam's voice breaks down to a whisper at the close, as he gazes down at the coffin of "a true wife". Four days after the funeral, Quilliam pays tribute to Fatima, ending with a poem, whose final stanza runs:

> 'Tis so our sister yielded
> The breath of mortal life;
> 'Tis so she ceased the struggle
> Of this fierce worldly strife;
> And saying, "it is over,"
> She winged her spirit flight.

Picture 5: The striking similarities between the young Hubert Haleem Cates-Quilliam (left) and the young Abdullah Quilliam (right).

At the Annual General Meeting of 1901, Quilliam went as close as he ever did to describing Fatima as a beloved, trusted wife in public. He said, making a daring allusion between himself and Fatima and the Prophet and Khadijah, that he "could almost say of her as the Prophet said of Khadijah, 'She believed in me and the Faith when all the world was against me.'" Fatima was the True Believer in the faith and one who did not doubt Quilliam's call to Islam, who stood steadfastly by his side when there were just a handful of converts, and who persevered despite the great harassment and viciousness she endured, both from street opponents of the Institute and from her violent, late husband, Hubert Cates.

It seems most likely that Quilliam conducted a private Islamic marriage with Fatima, most probably in July or August 1895, if they abided by the Islamic requirement that a widow should wait four months and ten days ('*idda*) before marrying another man. He was a fervent believer in polygamy and practised what he preached. At the time that Quilliam married Fatima in the summer of 1895, he had two other wives and families – with Hannah whom he married in 1879 and had four children with, and with Mary with whom he had four children at the time. He claimed to have married Mary according to Islamic rites, and gave a number of dates over the years, but they were only ever formally married in 1909 after Hannah's death. Hannah and Mary could not stand the sight of each other, according to the account of the Ottoman journalist, Yusuf Samih Asmay, who visited the mosque for a month in 1895. They lived in separate households, but would on rare occasions appear together at Institute functions.

On top of this, there were a lot of allegations in the mid-1890s about Quilliam's probity and character: he had his critics among his own Institute members, the Ottomans and the Indian Muslim activists in Britain. For example, a special meeting was held on 27 December 1896 by the London Anjuman-i-Islam to warn the Muslim public about what it saw as Quilliam's deep duplicity, spreading lies through his newspapers, feeding false information to the local press, and embezzling funds from the Muslim world under false pretences. The meeting featured testimonial speeches by former members of the Institute, Mustapha Khalil and Maulana Mohammad Barakatullah, the latter serving as the Institute's imam between 1893–6.

In this moment of heightened scrutiny, Quilliam's motive of self-preservation to keep his marriage to Fatima secret and to move her and his son away from the Muslim community and his two

Picture 6: A unique group photo of Quilliam with his family and some members of Liverpool Muslim Institute, dated circa 1893–5. It is possible that one of the two women sat on the right is Fatima Cates, but at present there are no positively identified photographs of her.

other families seems plain enough. It also seems fair to say that it was done to protect Fatima's reputation too. Fatima and Hubert Haleem ended up in West Kirby, a small coastal town on the far side of the Wirral, where she kept a boarding house. It was twenty miles from the Liverpool Muslim Institute, which she had helped to build from scratch with Quilliam from its first year in 1887. How must she have felt to have been sent away? Or, alternatively, was the removal from life in Liverpool more of a proactive choice on her part to get away from the complexities of Quilliam's family life? It is hard to say for sure, as her own voice disappears from the historical record after 1893. After that year, we are simply reading between the lines of Quilliam's narratives. What is harder to understand are Quilliam's reasons for eulogizing Hubert Cates in a poem upon

his death in 1895, given that he must have been privy to Cates'
murderous, violent abuse towards Fatima. While it could have been
due to his pastoral duties as a religious leader to all his congregation,
not all who passed in the community were eulogized in poetry or
described, as Cates was, as a "dear friend".

From what we can tell, Quilliam was an affectionate but
distant father to his son, Hubert Haleem. In the poem, "A Mother's
Lullaby", written two months after Hubert's birth, Quilliam writes:

> Two little blue eyes
>> Peering at mine
> Gazing so tenderly,
> Almost divine.
>> My Baby!
>
> [...]
>
> God, keep you darling
>> (He alone can.)
> To comfort your parents
>> When you are a man.
>> My Baby!

Hubert was sent away to a boarding school, the Lytham College
for Boys, in Lytham St-Annes, south of Blackpool. Like many a
doting father, Quilliam proudly announced the achievements
of Hubert as he did for his other children in his publications. In
1907, Hubert's role as head of sixth form is reported, and that he
is "a most satisfactory pupil", doing well at maths. Later on, when
Hubert serves on the Western Front in World War One, Quilliam
notes with relief that he is "back from the front" in 1920. Hubert's
military discharge photo, picturing him in his mid-twenties, shows
a remarkable likeness to Quilliam, showing him from 1893 when
he was in his mid-thirties (see Picture 5). Or the warm notice given
to the birth of Hubert's daughter, Winifred, in 1921, after Hubert
Haleem's marriage to Hannah Jackson (1895–1972) in 1920, when

he worked as a steamship steward. They also had a son, Hubert Allan Cates. Hubert Haleem served again during the Second World War when he won a medal for his maritime military service. Another big indication of Quilliam's fatherhood is that he named Hubert as an equal beneficiary in his will in 1932 alongside all his other surviving children. Hubert Haleem died of pneumonia in London in 1968 and was cremated.

Picture 7: Fatima's headstone installed 122 years after her death on Friday, 4 November 2022. The marble headstone features the last stanza of her poem and hymn, "A Moslimah's Prayer" (1892).

12

Fatima, Forgotten and Remembered

The Liverpool Muslim Institute closed its doors in 1908, shortly after Quilliam left the city because of a legal scandal in
which he was found out to have falsified evidence in a divorce case.
For years, it served as the registry for births, marriages and deaths in
the city. Files were kept in the extension and it was still called "the
mosque" by the staff but no one knew quite why.

Some communal memory of Quilliam and the Liverpool
Muslims did persist outside his immediate family, especially through
the British Muslim Society, which Quilliam joined as a member
when it was established in London in 1914, and then through its
offshoots among the small convert community in Britain right up
into the 1960s and beyond, particularly in the establishment of the
Association of British Muslims (est. 1976), which drew directly
on Quilliam's legacy, albeit one that was dimly remembered at the
time. The other conduit was the rediscovery of Abdullah Quilliam
and the Liverpool Muslim Institute by local Muslims in Liverpool
in the 1970s. This led eventually to the formation of the Abdullah

Quilliam Society in 1997, and to its procurement of 8–10 Brougham Terrace in 2000 from the Council. In 2014, it was reopened as a mosque after 106 years. Alongside this was a growing scholarly interest in Quilliam, with the first major biography of Quilliam and his community by Ron Geaves published in 2010, and this led to greater media coverage and public awareness of England's first mosque community.

Over time, attention has begun to shift away from a focus on Quilliam the individual towards understanding how the Liverpool Muslims worked as a small, pioneering convert community in touch with the wider Muslim world. In this shift, greater attention is now being paid towards the role of pioneering Muslimas in Britain's first mosque community by scholars such as Sariya Cheruvallil-Contractor, who points out that Fatima and Shahjehan played key roles in establishing Britain's first two mosques in Liverpool and Woking respectively. One of the authors of this biography, Maulana Hamid Mahmood, first heard of Fatima after buying Geaves' biography of Quilliam the day it came out in 2010. What he heard of her story inspired him to spend the following years researching her life further from primary sources. In December 2014, he established the Fatima Elizabeth Phrontistery, an Islamic supplementary school (madrasa) in northeast London. He wanted to name the madrasa after Fatima in honour of "the first lady ever converted to Islam in England", as the *Daily Dispatch* of Manchester described her charmingly but inaccurately in their obituary notice in 1900. As part of his research, Mahmood managed to locate Fatima's grave in Anfield Cemetery in February 2019, and found that it was unmarked. In April 2022, during Ramadan, a Liverpudlian Muslima convert, Amirah Scarisbrick, organized crowdfunding for a headstone to be placed at her grave for the first time. A marble headstone was installed on 4 November 2022. On 21 January

2023, a dozen convert associations from across the country came to pay their respects at Fatima's graveside and to remember together her life and work in co-founding Britain's first mosque community.

On the headstone was inscribed the final stanza of Fatima's seminal poem and hymn of 1892:

A faithful servant of Allah

Fatima Elizabeth Cates

1865–1900

Then may we ever heed,
The warning God has given,
That so we may in safety tread
The road that leads to Heaven

FEC 1892

Appendix I:
The Prose and Poetry of Fatima Cates

On the Folly of Heeding Scandal (1890)

The following page was written by our late sister, Mrs. Fatima E. Cates (whose demise we so recently chronicled) and was read before a meeting of the members of the Liverpool Muslim Institute during the session of 1890. It has never been previously printed:

So long as the race of men endures, the main occupation of the marvellous creatures after they have secured the means of subsistence will be to interest themselves in each other's business; and hence the true statements which we call "scandal" and the false ones which we call "slander" will always be scattered in plenty. A scandal may, of course, be false; but we use the word to signify any tale, true or false, which deals with the private or public conduct of any individual, and which represents that individual in a light the reverse of admirable. King Solomon and King David seem to have suffered bitterly at the hands of scandalmongers and slanderers, and they are equalled in bitterness only by the Patriarch Job; so, the antiquity of scandal is incontestable.

Shakespeare says very soundly that the most stainless of men and women must not expect to escape calumny; and we have an uncomfortable notion that the view taken by the world's greatest and wisest is very like the truth. We cannot remember one man in history and one man in the world of to-day who has not been made a mark for scandal. Cardinal Newman approached the saintly ideal as nearly as man may, and yet even he was once accused of using his position in order to lead the minds of young men astray. The Cardinal was a terrible disputant, and he effectually disposed of the scandal, but still it had been uttered. We were all agreed on calling the late Prince Consort "Albert the Good," and yet there was a time when that high-hearted man was the object of a storm of calumny, and his position in this country was regarded by some really shrewd men as rather precarious. We smile now at the reckless assaults which were made on the Prince; but people did not smite thirty-six years ago.

There are some modern men who enjoy scandal when it is directed against themselves, and actually invite it. They say, "I would rather have your spite than your pity," and they take the best possible means to secure the personal advertisement which reckless spite bestows on its object. These men generally manage to extract some personal profit from the keenest assaults made upon them, and they smile composedly while some unhappy enemy works himself into a perfect fury of earnestness. One celebrity was subjected to a long and most venomous series of assaults, and these were the deadliest ironies of a strong writer. The assailed person remained silent until the storm has abated, and then he sent round a paragraph which was widely printed. "It is not true that Mr. X. has paid any minor writer or writers to attack him." Only the forehead of brass could have endured the attack and remained unruffled.

So far as public men are concerned, we are used to hearing all kinds of violent accusations. A very prominent man's name may be printed a thousand times daily and dark charges made against him, yet if he remains perfectly quiet he takes no harm. If his private character be assailed, he is in peril, even though his offence may be trivial; but the very ecstasy of foul abuse does not alter his public position. Then there are the reformers – true and sham – who utter their convictions loudly. The sham should be denounced, but it always requires the keenest of eyes to distinguish truth from unreality, and hence we see man and women who are the very salt of the earth classed with charlatans and loaded with calumny. For the public character silence is the best retort, and it seems as if a steady, scornful refusal to answer any sort of accusation were far better than elaborate and logical defence. The cynical authors and dramatists sometimes profess great delights when their works are bitterly criticised; and they are certainly right in one particular, for an uncompromising attack on a book is sure to send up the sale, thanks to frail human nature. If a play becomes the subject of acrid discussion, the theatre is crowded; and hence some thick-skinned people will take incredible pains to invite attack, and they rejoice when the critic squirts gall and wormwood on them.

All this very curious, and perhaps entertaining, but it does not quite lie on the line of discussion which we want to follow. Most of those whom we address are not in need of fame or notoriety, and they are satisfied if they can pass through the world fulfilling duty honestly, feeling no might or overmastering emotions, and doing as little harm as possible while they pursue the even tenor of their way. Now, there are many of the good folk who fail to derive the highest pleasure from life, who fret themselves dismally only because they are eternally afraid of what the other people may be saying about them. We have never fairly gone into this subject by more than casual hints, and it seems to me wroth analysing from a few commonplace points of view. A large-minded, cool-tempered, clear-eyed man, who looks gently on the brothers of his race, and who knows his own weaknesses, cannot help being saddened by watching the uniform acrimony with which minds of low type are wont to criticise all the actions of others. All grades of society must be studied, and the observer must on no account allow temper to get the better of him. That calm and gentle mood which Marcus Antonius sought to make habitual among is the only proper state of mind in which to approach the study of the feeble and the fallen or falling; is it also the only safeguard when spite and envy and bitterness come suddenly before the eyes in all their repulsive varieties. Take this disposition to scandal in its lowest phases and observe how certain poor girls will chatter about each other, in season or out of season. With what certainty an evil tale finds its way round to the person about whom it is told, and how much pain it causes! Well, a good name is very precious to man or woman, just as good health; but an individual who is extravagantly querulous about the preservation of health ends by becoming a public nuisance; while the person who is for ever shrieking causelessly over tiny grievances is as great a pest as the sham invalid.

A certain lordly indifference may be easily assumed by those who have nerve enough for it; but is precisely the nerve the is oftenest wanting, and thus we have hundreds of harmless enough beings shivering over petty things which they imagine themselves to have done, and pettier things which they imagine other people to have said. We often have letters from sufferers who fancy that "everyone is looking at them," and it is difficult to say what should be done to remove that odd self-consciousness. Then there are others to whom the importance of outside opinion assumes tragic and terrific dimensions, so that they have few placid hours of life.

There are accusations which may be brought by an innuendo against such men as ministers and schoolmasters, and others whose position is delicate; and then the scandal is a matter of life and death. If there is only the whisper, the hint, the chuckle, then the marked victim can do very little save wait until he has something definite to catch at. If he takes too rapid action, and effectually disconcerts the scandalmongers, still the slain rumour leaves something harmful behind it. But if any definite word can be surely traced to one talker, then the fiercest measures should be taken, if necessary, to deal out punishment. Some good men have allowed a certain timidity to influence them. They have said "What is the good of fighting with a sweep?" and their sensitive delicacy has forbidden them to hurt a being against whom any legitimate weapon should have been unsparingly used. Then the old half-true saying, "There is no smoke without fire," has been quoted for the millionth time, and a man who in all probability had done no wrong remains under a slur. If the slandered individual has a good case, then the publicity of the widest kind should be invited, or rather, demanded, and the most defiant air should be deliberately assumed. A scandal of this vital sort is like an attempt to extort blackmail. Some silly and thin-skinned folk give way to the blackmailer to avoid trouble, and they thus hand themselves over to a cruel taskmaster, who shows no mercy; whereas, if they seized him on his first demand, and let him do his very worst, he would at once succumb like the cur that he is.

But our business is not with great scandals which blight lives and alters careers; we think rather of the petty tittle-tattle, which seems so trifling, and which causes such pain. Some grown men, strange to say, are absolutely miserable if they learn that someone has spoken disparagingly of them. But what on earth can a sneer or a piece of futile backbiting matter to any sane creature? Suppose, for example, that a man says he does not like you, that is a result of his peculiar temperament, and his dislike, however expressed, will hurt you no more than the breath of a summer breeze, so long as he is careful to keep outside the range of the law. It is the same with ordinary tittle-tattle. Women will come home from church in a perfect agony because they have seen that a whispered conversation was passing and fancied that they must be the subjects of it. The consciousness of being slightly inferior with regard to dress will haunt a silly person like a sense of crime; an innocent look from a passer-by is taken for insolent scrutiny, a vacant smile on the face of some merry girl is set down as an exhibition of insolence, and the poor self-tormentor often enters her own house and visits an outbreak of petulant temper on her own people. There are minds to which the amount of a neighbour's butcher's bill transcends all questions of imperial importance; there are minds capable of being occupied for an hour or a day or a week by the trilling fact that a lady has turned her last year's dress or has had an ancient sealskin done up. Then there are men of every rank – from the club aristocrat to the labourer in the taproom – who must needs tattle negative harmless stuff. The club man says the Jones is making a fool of himself by giving dinners which half poison people; Bob in the pothouse complains with acrimony that the absent Jemmy is never willing to pay his share, though he is most willing to pay his share, though he is most alert when it comes to drinking. Then look at the poor furious girls whose conversation is made up of "I says" and "she says," with tags of repeated scoldings.

The male backbiter and the female are alike not worth considering, and we are barely able to form a picture of the kind of mind which is influenced one way or another by such talk, which is, as it were, the soiled thistledown of speech. None the less we own that souls of really fine temper are hurt grievously by the cackle of the meanest and most ignoble of human creatures. Take the case of a poor, struggling professional man, whose stipend is sorely taxed by the demands of charity. He has to live meanly; his own wife's thin jacket offers a chilly contrast to the lordly sealskin worn by the wife of his butcher; his own boots show an obtrusive patch, and the high-bred scholar sometimes is driven nearly distraught by the certain knowledge that the butcher, the baker, the churchwarden, the innkeeper, all discuss his poverty with malice, or, at least, with a careless contempt, which is worse still. The man cannot help the way in which he has been trained; vulgar gossip strikes him like a blow, and he is indeed to be pitied. But why should he not brace him up to indifference? Could he only rigidly force his own intellect to perceive that he is none the worse for all the babble of village or town he might be nearly happy; as it is, he passes sleepless nights in imagining what may possibly be said to him by the lowest of the low, and he scourges himself with remorse when he thinks of the straits to which he has brought his partner. There would be no harm done by a little airy heedlessness in this instance, and in such a way many an essentially noble soul might be rescued from self-torture. Just one consideration must be pressed on reasonable readers at this juncture. We ask, "Do you know that the very people who gabble spitefully concerning you are those who fawn most fulsomely on you when they meet you face to face?" Supposing that you suddenly enter a room where people have been talking about you, there is something in the air, there is an indefinable and indescribable expression on the face of the talkers, and you know what has been passing. One of the gossips may sulk and look embarrassed, but the identical person who has most freely decried you is cordial, and even affectionate. Since that chatter is of a kind which is too small or too base to be repeated in your hearing, why notice it? In the North of England there is a delightful word used to describe the efforts of gossips; the scandal is called "clash," and the term is effective. To the low mind, miserable, personal gossip is an essential of contentment, and such talk is "clash" – a noise and nothing more. Women of the "clashing" sort are abhorred and avoided by all quiet and sensible people; they frame their little stories, they vent their little criticisms, and no more is to be said. If they take a genuine spit against a young girl, they may vary her life by some amount of small annoyance; but, if the girl has a will and nerve, she may not only neglect the gossips, but she may absolutely terrorise them into discretion. As to the thin, vain scandal which creeps into print, and perhaps hurts sensitive skins as if spurts of a biting acid had been thrown on them, it has its minute or its hour, and the man or woman who notices it should be put under control at once.

It is no pleasant task to us when we have to say something regarding the meanness of man's nature; but when we see that things unimportant are treated as important, that things which should be laughed at are allowed to give pain, we think it advisable to endeavour to employ a little clear common sense to defend sensitive persons from their own too amiable weakness.

The Marriage Question (April 1891)

Liverpool Mercury, 16 Apr 1891.

To the Editors of the Liverpool Mercury.

Gentlemen, – Your correspondent "Esperanza" in one of her recent letters recommended one of your other correspondents to join the Moslem Church of Liverpool, as their views with reference to the control of wives would be more in accordance with his, and thereby insinuated that the state of the marriage laws amongst Mahommedans was even more unsatisfactory than in Christian England.

This is one of the vulgar errors into which persons whose whole knowledge of Mahommedanism is derived from reading books and pamphlets written by bigoted Christian missionaries and others, so often fall into. Therefore permit me, as a Moslem lady and wife, to at once say that Mahommedan ladies enjoy, and have done so ever since the time of the Prophet, much greater legal rights as to separate property, divorce than those enjoyed by Christians up to quite a recent date.

The Mahommedan lady on marriage does not lose her personality, and is entitled to hold property in her own right to a far greater extent than married females in this country are allowed even under the various Married Women's Property Acts that have emanated from the Legislature within the last 25 years. Space will not permit me to give instances of these; but if your correspondent will study the article by the vice-president of our institute (Rafiuddeen Ahmed) which appeared in the last number of the *Asiatic Quarterly Review*, she will find the whole subject dealt with most exhaustively. And now with regard to the marriage question. The whole and sole trouble in connection with the marriage and divorce laws in this country is that they are modelled upon Christian ideas, and that marriage partakes to a greater or less degree of a religious ceremony. A calm consideration of the history of our marriage laws will show this to any unbiased student. Firstly, we find that England was primarily a Catholic country, and the Catholic Church regarded marriage as a sacrament and did not permit divorce. Then came the Protestant Reformation. Marriage was still looked upon as a part and portion of Christian worship, and divorce could only be obtained by means of a private Act of Parliament – a most expensive process. Then came the jurisdiction of the ecclesiastical courts in matters of divorce and then finally the Divorce Act of 1857, which shook off many of the shackles of priestly interference, but still retained some of the objectionable features of the marriage law, purely the outcome of Christianity. What is required to remedy this evil is to at once and for ever, get rid of the notion that marriage is in any way bound up with religion, and to regard it solely and wholly as a civil contract between two parties, entered into with their mutual consent, due care being always taken that the interests of any children there may be as issues of such marriage may be protected. This is the key of the whole difficulty.

Fatima E. Cates.

5th Ramazan A.H. 1308

Liverpool Mercury, 17 Apr 1891

To the Editors of the Liverpool Mercury.

Gentlemen, – I find that a sentence has been accidentally omitted in my letter of yesterday's date. The last paragraph should read as follows:

"What is required to remedy this evil is to regard marriage solely and wholly as a civil contract between two parties, entered into with their mutual consent and which by the like mutual consent can be also dissolved, due care being always taken that the interests of any children there may be as issue of such marriage may be protected. This is the key of the whole difficulty."

Fatima E. Cates.

6th Ramazan A.H. 1306

How I Became A Mahommedan (September 1891)

When I was a girl about 19 years of age, I used frequently to attend Temperance meetings, and it was at one of these meetings I heard Mr. Quilliam, who is well-known in Liverpool as a great advocate of Total Abstinence, deliver a lecture on "Fanatics and Fanaticism," in which he gave a very graphic account of the early struggles of our holy prophet Mahomet. Up to this time I had always heard about Mahomet described as an imposter and a blood-thirsty man, who forced people to believe in his religion by threatening to put them to death, if they did not do so. I was of course much astonished at hearing Mr. Quilliam giving a different account of him.

I waited until the end of the meeting, and I then asked Mr. Quilliam to tell me something more of this religion, as I was very much in doubt as to the true faith. He spoke to me for some time; in fact he gave me a short sketch of the main principles of Islam and offered to lend me his Koran in order that I could read it for myself saying, "Don't believe what I say, or what anyone else says; study the matter out for yourself."

I thanked him and a few days afterwards Mr. Quilliam gave me the Koran. I accordingly took it home and commenced carefully reading it. My mother who is a most bigoted Christian, on perceiving this asked me what I was reading. I answered, "The Mahommedan Bible." She replied angrily, "How dare you read such a vile and wicked book? Give it to me this moment and let me burn it. I will not allow such trash to be in my house." I answered, "No I will not, how can I know whether it is a wicked book or not until I have read it?" She tried to take the book from me, but I escaped to my bedroom and locked myself in and went on reading, what I now consider the most precious book that could be bought.

I was continually scolded and threatened with all kinds of punishments if I continued to read such a book, but all to no purpose; for I persisted in reading it, and finally I had to carry the Koran about with me, or during my absence it would have been destroyed.

I then told Mr. Quilliam I would attend his meetings if I might; he replied, "I could do so if I wished," and of course I did. At that time the only Musulmans in Liverpool were Mr. Quilliam and Mr. Hamilton. We

85

used to meet, we three, week after week, and read the Koran and discuss matters. It was with great difficulty I managed to attend these meetings, being constantly watched, or occasionally by way of a change, shut up in a room to prevent my going, as they did not wish me to become a Moslem, having been strictly brought up in the orthodox Christian faith; and it was because I declared my views contrary to theirs on Christianity, that they thought I was being led away to some other faith, probably Roman Catholicism, which they held in abhorrence; but on finding it to be the Islamic faith words could not express their surprise and indignation. To their ideas it was even worse, for they told me I was entirely lost, and no possible hope of salvation for my soul, unless I returned to my former belief. I then declared myself a Moslem and it was then that all kinds of devices were resorted to, to prevent my attending the meetings. If I wrote, my letters were intercepted, and no one can conceive the satire and ridicule I had to endure from them up to the present which is now about five years.

When Mr. Quilliam first began lecturing on Mahommedanism, we used to meet in a little room, the entrance to which was up a flight of stairs in a side street, and the neighbours used to come and jeer at us, and sometimes they amused themselves by throwing stones and other filthy garbage at us, as we entered or left the room in which we held our meetings.

It was very hard work at first, but we went on steadily, then another convert was made, Mr. Wardle, then Mr. Smith, and gradually others; but for about twelve months I was the only lady that attended. Now we have a nice little mosque fairly comfortably furnished, but the mob still annoy us by throwing mud and stones; however we persevere, and are still making fresh converts.

About three years ago I was married to a gentleman I was affianced to prior to becoming a Moslem. My husband was then a Christian just as prejudiced and bigoted as my mother, and their views being the same both tried to keep me from the mosque, but in vain. He seeing I was still determined to follow it up, and thinking there must be some truth in it, commenced likewise to read the Koran, then to attend the lectures, and finally, I am happy to say, he has become one of the votaries of our faith.

A little over nine months ago a younger sister of mine came to reside with me. She like myself had been brought up, indoctrinated with all the tenets of the Orthodox Church of England Christian faith. After she had been with me some few weeks she expressed a desire to attend one of the public lectures that we hold in the lecture hall of our Moslem Institute. The lecturer was Mr. Quilliam, and he took for his subject "Fables of ancient times," and pointed out to the audience how all religions, except Islam, had become corrupted by the addition of silly myths and traditions, and shewed how much simpler and purer the faith of Islam was than that of other creeds.

When we got home my sister remarked how easy it was to understand and follow such a lecture, and how different it was to the dry and uninteresting theological discourses she had heard in Christian Churches and stated she would like to hear more about Islam. The result was that in the course of about three months she also became a Moslem. I could give other instances of how conversions have been made, but will content myself with simply relating those I have given above as they refer to my own family; but probably in another article I will express my views as to how the work of proselytising could be most successfully carried on amongst females and children in England.

Fatima E. Cates

September 11th, 1891.

Liverpool Moslem Institute.

A Moslimah's Prayer (September 1891)

Beset by numerous foes,
Concealed along the way,
We must those enemies oppose,
And ever work and pray.

They watch but to devour,
Like ravening beasts of prey,
If we in an unguarded hour,
But cease to work and pray.

Then may we ever heed,
The warning God has given,
That so we may in safety tread
The road that leads to Heaven.

Fatima E. Cates,

2 Marmaduke Street, Liverpool

The Liverpool Converts: Correct Details (1892)

As some Indian Papers have published Lists professing to be a complete account of the converts in Liverpool, and these reports have mostly been incorrect, incomplete and unauthorised I think it wise to give your readers a full and correct list of the members of the Liverpool Moslem Institute mentioning their profession and their former religion. I may also mention that the signature of each of these persons duly appears in the Member's Allegiance book of the Liverpool Society appended to the following declaration.

"We the undersigned hereby acknowledge our belief in the Moslem Faith and that we hold the same and none other to be the true religion and that we believe:
1. That there is only one God.
2. That Mahommed is his prophet.
3. That the Koran is the inspired Book and word of God."

Since compiling this list I have deemed it necessary to separate it into 4 divisions. The first contains the names of the adult converts in order of their conversion; the second division contains the names of the children of the members; the third division gives the names of born Moslem members of the association; and the fourth list contains the names of former members who have died.

List 1.

	Names.	*Profession.*	*Former Religion.*
1	William Henry Quilliam.	Solicitor.	Wesleyan Christian.
2	James Ali Hamilton.	Wholesale Boxmaker.	Church of England.
3	Fatima Cates.	Married.	Church of England.
4	William U. Wardle.	Clerk in the Ottoman Consulate	Unitarian Christian.
5	George Khalid Smith.	Detective.	Church of England.
6	John Lester.	Financial Agent.	Church of England.
7	Julia Lester.	Married.	Wesleyan.
8	Alfred Reignier.	Professor of Languages.	Catholic Priest.
9	Alice Bertha Bowman.	Authoress.	Church of England.
10	Clement Caulton.	Master Builder.	Spiritualist.
11	Thomas Omar Byrne.	Shorthand Writer.	Catholic.
12	John Owen Quilliam.	Cashier and book-keeper [to] W.H. Quilliam	Wesleyan.
13	Fanny Brown.	Widow.	Church of England.
14	Michael Hall.	Master Tailor.	Methodist.
15	Emily L. Thomas.	Spinster.	Catholic.
16	Tom Power.	Insurance Agent.	Catholic.
17	Henry Brooks.	Cabinet Maker.	Church of England.
18	Agnes B. Elliot.	Married.	Church of England.
19	William Bird.	Pilot.	Church of England.
20	Hubert Henry Cates.	Chief Marine Engineer.	Church of England.
21	Charles E. Power.	Surgeon.	Church of England.

22	Alma Power.	Married.	Jewess.
23	Arthur Radford.	Plumber.	Salvation Army.
24	Isabella Moran.	Spinster.	Catholic.
25	Clara Haleema Murray.	Spinster.	Church of England.
26	William Hughes Quilliam.	Accountant.	United Methodist Free Church.
27	George Francis Cuss.	Hotel Proprietor.	Atheist.
28	Paul Harrison.	Teacher of Music.	Swedenburgian Christian.
29	Helen Karsa.	Married.	Church of England.
30	Charles Falkner.	Professor of Languages and Mathematics, graduate of the University.	Protestant Southern Church.
31	J. Devereux Pugh.	Solicitor of the Supreme Court.	Church of England.
32	Elizabeth Pugh.	Married.	Church of England.
33	Hugh H. Johnston.	B.A. (Oxon) M.R.I.A.	Formerly Clergyman of the Church of England.
34	Walter Lowe.	Solicitor's Articled Clerk.	Church of England.
35	Hannah Rodda Robinson Shah.	Married.	Church of England.
36	Amelia Davies.	Married.	Jewess.
37	Margaret Jones.	Spinster.	Salvation Army.
38	Leah Banks.	Housekeeper.	Wesleyan.
39	Louisa H. Jones.	Housekeeper.	Wesleyan.
40	Matthew Rainbow.	Mercantile Clerk.	Presbyterian.
41	Mrs. Mary Quilliam.	Married.	Christian.

Children of Members.

1. Robert Ahmed Quilliam. 2. William Henry Abdullah [Billal] Quilliam. 3. Elizabeth Chadijah Quilliam. 4. Harriet Hanifa Quilliam. 5. Bianca Hamilton. 6. Ernest Hamilton. 7. William Robert Brown. 8–12. Five children of Mrs. Robinson-Shah, whose names I do not know as they have gone to Turkey. 13. Ethel Mariam Quilliam. 14. Lillian Aiyesha Quilliam. 15. Henry Mahomed Quilliam. 16. Florence Zulieka Quilliam.

Born Mussulmans.

1. His Excellency Ismail Loutfy Bey, Ottoman Consul General Liverpool. 2. Rafiuddin Ahmad, Bar Student. 3. Abdur Rasul, Bar Student. 4. Mohamed Ahmed, Bar Student. 5. Syed Abdul Halim, Bar Student. 6. Hafiz Abdul Rahim. 7. Ismail Ibrahim Azeem. 8. Mustapha Karsa, Merchant. 9. Golab Shah, Oculist. 10. Sheikh Meeran Bux, Student. 11. Agha Zade Mehmed, Carpet Merchant. 12. Karim O-Glau Halil, Merchant. 13. Abdullah O-Glau Ibrahim. 14. Mustafa O-Glau Cherif, Merchant. 15. H. Azimuddin, Student.

Deaths.

1. Bahr Edris, formerly of Egypt died 29th March, 1891. 2. David Grundy, England died July 1891. 3. Budhasa Lagos West Africa died 27th November, 1891.

Summary.

English Adult Converts	40
English Children	16
Born Moslems	15
Deaths	3
Total since Foundation	74

Khadija (1893)

How can the feeble pen express,
How can the poet praise,
Thy noble acts of righteousness,
Thy virtuous deeds and ways?
Thou ruler of this happy State,
Thou noble Shahjahan fair;
How can this humble bard relate
Thy virtues, bright and rare?
Mercy, and Truth, and Equity,
Combine to spread thy fame;
As while thy magnanimity
Thy great soul doth proclaim!
With grateful hearts our thoughts we raise
Towards Heaven, in earnest prayer
That happiness and length of days
May be thy blessed share!

F. E. C.

Appendix II: Key Documents

Divorce Petition (1891)

14745

In the High Court of Justice Probate Divorce and Admiralty Division (Divorce)

Cates

V

Cates

Affidavit in Support of Petition for Dissolution of Marriage

101—

FILED 16 DEC 1891

M. Nordon
Solicitor
23 Wormwood Street
London E.C.
Petitioners Solicitor

In the High Court of Justice Probate Divorce and Admiralty Division (Divorce)

The 15th day of December 1891.

To the Right Honourable the President of the said Division Cause No.

The Humble Petition of Francess Elizabeth Cates of 2 Marmaduke Street Edge Hill in the City of Liverpool in the County of Lancaster. Wife of Hubert Henry Cates of the said City Marine Chief Engineer.

Sheweth:

1. That your petitioner then Francess Elizabeth Murray was on the 28th day of February 1889 lawfully married to the said Hubert Henry Cates at the Cathedral Church of St Peters in the said City.

2. That after her said marriage your petitioner lived and cohabited with her said husband at 96 Newcombe Street, Anfield, near Liverpool aforesaid and subsequently at 45 Adelaide Road and at 2 Marmaduke Street both in Liverpool aforesaid and that there has never been any issue of the said marriage.

3. That the said Hubert Henry Cates is a man of violent and uncontrollable temper and in the habit of using foul disgusting and filthy language and oaths unprecautious and threats of personal violence and that he has upon diverse occasions struck and violently beaten and assaulted your petitioner and has caused her great pain and injury both physical and mental and seriously impaired her health.

4. That shortly after the said marriage while living in Newcombe Street aforesaid namely in or about the month of June 1889 on one occasion the said Hubert Henry Cates to terrify and annoy your Petitioner after using most foul and disgusting language took up a pair of brass fire tongs and, with them in the presence of your Petitioner (she being alone with him in the house) smashed several pictures then hanging on the wall and threatened to also smash your Petitioner's head with the said tongs in consequence whereof your Petitioner swooned away and was unconscious for several hours.

5. That while living in Newcombe Street aforesaid in order to further terrify, vex and annoy your petitioner, the said Hubert Henry Cates on two occasions threatened and actually attempted to commit suicide by swallowing poison.

6. That on another occasion while living in Newcombe Street aforesaid namely on or about the 21st day of March 1890 the said Hubert Henry Cates beat and abused your petitioner and struck her two violent blows on the head and locked her in a portion of the house and threatened her with other violence.

Your Petitioner however escaped from the house and fearing further violence sought refuge at the residence of a mutual friend that subsequently namely on or about the 24th day of March 1890 an agreement of separation was drawn up between and signed by your Petitioner and the said Henry Hubert Cates whereby they mutually agreed in the future to live separate and apart.

7. That in or about the month of March 1890 and at diverse other times the said Hubert Henry Cates committed adultery with one Maggie Butler sometimes called Maggie Baker in a house of ill fame, Number 5, Ardcorak Hardinger Street, in the said City of Liverpool.

8. That after living apart from the said Hubert Henry Cates pursuant to the agreement for separation set forth in Paragraph 6 hereof your Petitioner consented to resume cohabitation with the said Hubert Henry Cates on his making many promises of amendment and future good behaviour and expressing great contrition for his past conduct but such cohabitation was only resumed on the express condition that your petitioner should occupy a separate bedroom from the said Hubert Henry Cates for a period of six months from the date of resumption of such cohabitation.

9. That subsequently while residing at 2, Marmaduke Street aforesaid namely in or about the month of February 1891, your Petitioner was again assaulted and beaten by the said Hubert Henry Cates who locked your Petitioner and himself in her bedroom on which occasion the said Hubert Henry Cates seized your Petitioner by both wrists and forcing her down bruised her arms very badly causing great discoloration of the flesh and grievous bodily pain and used dire threats of further violence against her and threatened to kill her and your petitioner in order to escape his violence was obliged to break several panes of glass in the window in order

to attract the attention of the other persons in the house whereby your petitioner's hands were cut and severely hurt.

10. That on another occasion the said Hubert Henry Cates came to your petitioner while she was undressed in bed and holding a table knife to her throat threatened to cut her throat and was with great difficulty prevented from doing so.

11. That on many occasions in public places the said Hubert Henry Cates has publicly insulted your petitioner by in a loud and angry tone of voice using vile and insulting epithets towards her and telling her " to go to Hell" to the great annoyance and vexation of mind of your petitioner and to the injury of her reputation.

12. That on the 7th day of December 1891 at 2, Marmaduke Street, Liverpool, aforesaid the said Hubert Henry Cates assaulted and beat your petitioner and struck her a violent blow on the side of the head causing the blood to flow from her ear and subsequently picked up a heavy iron fire iron rest of the weight of 2 lbs or thereabouts and threatened to "brain" your Petitioner and raising the said weapon attempted to strike your petitioner therewith but was prevented from doing so by the sister of your Petitioner in consequence whereof your Petitioner laid an information against the said Hubert Henry Cates in the Petty Sessional Court for the said City and on the 9th day of December 1891 the said summons came on for hearing before W.J. Stewart Esq., Stipendiary Magistrate for the City of Liverpool, at the Police Courts, Dale Street, Liverpool aforesaid when the said Hubert Henry Cates pleaded guilty to an aggravated assault upon your petitioner and an order was made by the court for judicial separation and the said Hubert Henry Cates was mulcted in a fine for the offence and was bound over in his own recognizances in £20 to keep the peace for the period of 12 months thence next ensuing.

13. That since the making of such order for judicial separation as mentioned in the last preceding paragraph hereof the said Hubert Henry Cates has made many threats of violence against your Petitioner and she has been obliged to place herself under police protection.

14. That during the years 1889, 1890, and 1891 the said Hubert Henry Cates has also committed adultery at Liverpool aforesaid with a woman called "Alice" but whose full name is unknown by your Petitioner.

Your Petitioner therefore humbly prays your Lordship to decree that her marriage with the said Hubert Henry Cates may be dissolved and that, your Petitioner may have such further and other relief in the premises as may seem just.

Frances E. Cates

Death of Sister Fatima Elizabeth Cates (1900)

It is our melancholy duty to announce the somewhat sudden demise of one who took a very prominent position in the early propaganda of the Islamic cause in England, namely, our sister Fatima Elizabeth Cates. It will probably be within the recollection of those who have studied the rise and progress of Islam in England that the first converts were obtained by means of public lectures, which was delivered by Sheikh Abdullah Quilliam, and it was by this means that our late sister became connected with and converted to the faith. In the spring of 1887, the Sheikh gave a lecture under the auspices of a society called the "Liverpool Temperance League," at Vernon Hall, Liverpool, and through that address secured his first convert – Bro. J. Ali Hamilton. On the following Wednesday, the Sheikh gave the same discourse, under the auspices of Birkenhead Workingmen's Temperance Association, in the Queen's Hall, Birkenhead, and among his audience was a young lady who was officially connected with the society named, and also with the Good Templar Order in Cheshire. By a happy fortune Bro. Ali Hamilton was also amongst the audience, and was seated next to the lady in question. During the progress of the lecture the lady evinced the greatest interest in what the speaker was saying, and, whilst the lecturer was being heartily applauded at the conclusion of his address, she happened to turn to Bro. Ali Hamilton and remark, "I never knew that Mahammedans were teetotalers. I should like to know something more about their religion." Bro. Ali Hamilton, with all the ardour of a new convert, commenced to explain Islam to her, and begged of her to speak to the Sheikh at the close of the meeting, and ask him for further particulars. This she did, and, in order to explain Islam fully, the Sheikh lent her his Koran and wrote a short explanatory treatise for her with reference to the faith. His letters to her were afterwards extended into a lecture, and subsequently published in book form, and issued under the title of "The Faith of Islam," while the lecture he had delivered, and which secured him his two first converts was also published in book form under the title of "Fanatics and Fanaticism." In the month of June, the converts had increased to four, and then the first Muslim society in England was instituted, Mr. Quilliam being chosen president, Mr. Hamilton secretary and Mrs. Cates treasurer. Meetings were held every Friday for prayers and reading and studying the Koran, and another meeting was arranged for Sunday evenings for public lectures to explain the faith. At all of these meetings Sister Cates, then Sister Murray, was a constant attendant, and she soon made herself felt as an earnest worker for Islam. It is impossible to describe the manner in which these Islamic converts were derided, the insults and indignities to which they were subjected and the personal violence that was ofttimes used against them. The windows of the little hall in which they held their meetings were repeatedly broken with stones, and roughs and Christian bigots frequently entered the room and made disturbances therein; while, in the street, the Muslims were stoned and pelted with decayed vegetable matter and rotten eggs, and followed by a crowd shouting after them. On several occasions, ruffians, unworthy of the name of men, lifted up horse manure from the road and rubbed it over our late sister's face. She endured it all, despite the fact that at the time every member of her family was bitterly opposed to her attending the meetings, and were horrified at the thought that she should have rejected Christianity. Time rolled on, and by the February of 1889, the little band had increased to 20 members, among other converts being the Rev. David Grundy, formerly of the primitive Methodist communion; and Sister Cates had induced a young man, to whom she was afterwards married, to also declare himself a Muslim. Her husband, Bro. Hubert Haleem Cates, was a marine chief engineer, making fortnightly trips between Liverpool and Lisbon, in Portugal, and he manifested a lively interest in Islamic work, and Muslim visitors to Liverpool were often entertained at their house. The first Indian students who came to England boarded with her. In process of time a younger sister of Mrs. Cates became a convert to Islam, and was, later on, married to a young Muslim gentleman Syed Abdul Haleem, and she is at present residing with her husband in India, and we believe their union has been most happy and been blessed with three children. Another sister of Mrs. Cates also married an Indian gentleman, a barrister-at-law, and she has one child. Up to the time of his death, which occurred in the month of January, 1896, Bro. Cates always attended the services at the mosque throughout the periods he was on shore, and he read several papers before the Literary and Debating Society, his wife taking a deep interest in the work. The union was only blessed with one child, a boy, who was born about 5 months after his father's death, and who is now, therefore, left parentless. After her husband's death Mrs. Cates removed to West Kirby, where she supported herself and her son by keeping a boarding house and letting furnished apartments. For the last two years she did not enjoy good health, and in consequence of the distance she lived out of town, and the necessity of attending to her household duties, she did not visit the mosque regularly, but her interest in the same never flagged, and she painted a very beautiful vase, ornamenting it with flowers and a text from the Koran, and presented it to the Institution. This gift stands at present on the platform in the lecture hall.

Some ten days prior to her demise she contracted a severe cold, and on Wednesday, October 24, was too ill to leave her bedroom. At the time it was not contemplated anything was seriously the matter with her beyond an attack of influenza. On Saturday, the 27th ultimo, she was very much worse, and medical aid was called in, but next day she appeared to be much better. On the Monday morning, however, acute pneumonia supervened, and at three o'clock the doctor pronounced that there was no hope. Telephonic message was at once sent to the Sheikh-ul-Islam, who proceeded to the house. Sister Cates was perfectly conscious, and expressed to him her wish to be buried as a Muslim, as she would die in Faith she had embraced, and further desired him to conduct the funeral service over her grave, and to be guardian to her little boy. Half an hour later she expired.

A few moments before she died our sister raised the index finger of her right hand, and slowly, but clearly, repeated the Kaleema in Arabic, then putting her hand in that of the Sheikh, she smiled a sweet smile and said, "Goodbye; it is all over," and without a struggle peacefully yielded up her breath.

The Funeral (1900)

The funeral of Mrs. Cates took place at Anfield Cemetery, Liverpool, on October 31 [1900], and as this was the first interment of a Muslim in those grounds, a not inconsiderable number of Christians assembled to witness the proceedings. The story of the deceased's unostentatiously useful and devout life did not seem to be unknown, and on every hand there were manifestations of pungent grief and unrestrained sympathy. Conventionalities were conspicuous by their absence. There was no long procession of expensive broughams drawn by silver-bedecked horses; no clamouring crowd anxious to advertise their presence; no carriage laden with a wealth of flowers intended to convey feelings of condolence. Everything was simple, quiet, but beautifully imposing and impressive, and the tout ensemble acted upon non-Muslims as had nothing previously in their recollection. The obsequies were performed just within the mosque portals and at the graveside in Arabic and English by the Sheikh (Abdullah Quilliam Effendi), and the prayers offered before the committal service were repeated by a company of little fellows from the Medina Home, who were in care of Captain J. Omar Lester.

It is impossible to depict the scene as it presented itself. The Sheikh was in attendance in what may be coldly described as his official capacity. He was also there as the man who received the deceased lady into the faith, who throughout his valiant struggle for Islam was ever loyally aided by the woman whose soul had returned to its maker, and who grasped the kind hand and comforted the pure and holy mind of the beloved creature in the awful moments of transition. Mrs. Cates' husband was one of the warmest friends of the Sheikh, who watched the career of her child with all the affection and pride of a loving guardian.

Stern winter had lain her relentless hand on the charming flowers and shrubs, and as the cortege made its way slowly along the cemetery path the grounds seemed encompassed with a misty halo as though harmonising with the sorrow of relatives and friends, who found words inadequate to express their feelings. The inspiring, pathetic, yet hopeful recitation by the tomb held the group spellbound, and as the Sheikh plaintively uttered the closing syllables his voice became almost inaudible, and the atmosphere was filled with a reverent solemnity that overcame the sensations. The

Sheikh gazed down on the thin, plain coffin which encased the remains of a pious woman, a true wife, an adoring mother – remains of a woman who had fulfilled, if ever one did, God's mission on Earth; the tiny, parentless boy stood awed by the brink of the grave; the fond and aged mother sobbed and trembled as the daughter's corpse disappeared – there were a few dry eyes, but only a few. The chief mourners included Mrs. Murray (mother of deceased), Master Haleem Cates (son), Mr. C. and Mrs. Duckett (brother-in-law and sister), the misses Polly and Aggie Murray (sisters), Mrs. Ghoosh (sister) and Miss Enid Ghoosh (niece), Mr. And Mrs. W. Ismail Winter, Master Miss Winter, Mrs. Bertha Amina Smith, Dr. H. Mustapha Léon and Professor H. Nasrullah Warren, F.S.O.

The Sheikh's Tribute to the Memory of the Deceased (1900)

On Sunday evening last the Sheikh-ul-Islam of the British Isles (Abdullah Quilliam Effendi) delivered a most touching oration at the mosque, which was crowded with an earnest congregation of sympathising Muslims. Taking for his subject, "Our Departed Friends," the Sheikh gave a graphic sketch of the lives of Mr. Thomas Ridpath and of our late Sister Fatima E. Cates, both of whom departed their mortal life upon the same day. The Sheikh then proceeded to deliver an exposition of Islamic views with regard to what is termed death, and pointed out how the true-believer could never be dismayed at death, but rather regarded it as a happy stage of his existence, it being the period when the Muslim, through the mercy of Allah, flung away the toils of the world and entered into eternal rest and peace. The sheikh concluded his eloquent and pathetic panegyric by reciting the following beautiful and original verses, composed by him that afternoon:

> We have passed the noonday summit,
> We have left the noonday heat,
> And down the hillside slowly
> Descend our wearied feet.
> Yet the evening air is balmy,
> And the evening shadows sweet.

Our summer's latest roses
Lay withered long ago;
And e'en the flowers of autumn
Scarce keep their mellowed glow.
Yet a peaceful season woos us,
Ere the time of storms and snow,

Like the tender twilight weather
When the toil of day is done;
And we feel the bliss of quiet
Our constant hearts have won,
When the vesper planet blushes,
Kissed by the dying sun.

So falls that tranquil season,
Dew-like, on soul and sight;
Faith's silvery star-rise blended
With memory's sunset light,
Wherein life pauses softly
Along the verge of night.

'Tis so our sister yielded
The wreath of mortal life;
'Tis so she ceased the struggle
Of this fierce worldly strife;
And, saying, "It is over,"
She winged her spirit flight.

The large audience was visibly affected by the Sheikh's feeling address, and scarcely a dry eye was to be seen.

The utmost sympathy is manifested by the Muslims towards the family of the deceased.

May Allah rest her soul in eternal peace!

Picture 8: The promotional flyer for Commemoration of Fatima Cates on 21 January 2023, organised by twelve convert associations around Britain.

The Commemoration of Fatima Elizabeth Cates (2023)

(Correct at the time of going to press.)

**Fatima Elizabeth Cates Commemoration,
Saturday 21 January 2023
Anfield Cemetery and the Abdullah Quilliam Mosque
Hosts: Abdullah Quilliam Society plus 13 UK Convert
Associations**

Programme

9.00

Arrival at Anfield Cemetery
238 Priory Rd, Anfield, Liverpool L4 2SL
Officiant – Sheikh Abdul Aziz Fredericks
Prayers & Quran readings at graveside

9.30

Depart Anfield Cemetery
Arrival at Quilliam Village/Old West Derby Union (10–15 minutes drive) 1–7, Brougham Terrace, L6 1AE, next to the old mosque at 8–10.

12.00 – 1.15

Meet and Greet/Lunch 12.30

1.15 – 1.30

Welcome from Host – Amanda Morris (Cardiff New Muslims)

Welcome from Abdullah Quilliam Society Chair – Ghalib Khan

Quran recitation – Shaykh Waddah Saleh

1.30 – 2.00   Book launch of *Our Fatima of Liverpool – The Story of Fatima Elizabeth Cates, The Victorian woman who helped found British Islam.* PowerPoint Presentation – Maulana Hamid Mahmood and Yahya Birt

2.00 – 2.30   Dhuhr followed by Asr Prayer 02.13pm – led by Sheikh Bilal Brown

2.30 – 3.00   *The Importance of Muslima Converts in Britain* – Chair: Batool Al-Toma / Amirah Scarisbrick /Shaykha Aisha Bewley / Dr. Sariya Cheruvallil-Contractor (7 minutes each)

3.00 – 3.30   An Historical Overview of England's First Mosque by Prof. Ron Geaves/includes video presentation

3.30 – 3.45   Storytelling – The Perseverance of Fatima – Sister Jumana Moon

Choir / poetry – Shaykha Marzuqa Karimah and Fatima Elizabeth Choir from the Fatima Elizabeth Phrontistery

A Moslimah's Prayer (1892) by Fatima Cates

Anthem for the Prophet's Birthday (1896) by Abdullah Quilliam

3.45 – 4.30	Refreshments: Tea – Coffee – Socialising/ Networking.

This function is primarily one that is hoped will strengthen the bonds of the convert community across the whole of the UK by means of linking together different associations, jamaats and communities.

Short tours of England's first mosque (by rotation with expert guides)

Concluding address and closing du'a – Shaykh Abdalhaqq Bewley

16.34   **Maghrib & Isha' Prayers**

17.00 – 18.00   Depart

*****

Steering Group Members:

Abdur Raheem Green (iERA)
Aliya Quadri (CEO, Solace UK)
Hajj Amal Douglas (Ihsan Mosque, Norwich)
Aminah Morris (Cardiff New Muslims)
Amirah Scarisbrick (Fundraiser for FEC's headstone)
Batool Al-Toma (Convert Muslim Foundation; Commemoration organiser)
Sheikh Bilal Brown (New Beginnings)
Bilal Harrison (Leeds New Muslims)
Maulana Hamid Mahmood (Fatima Elizabeth Phrontistery and FEC expert)

Kerry Mannan (Luton Revert Group)
Mumin Khan (CEO, Abdullah Quilliam Society)
Prof. Ron Geaves (Abdullah Quilliam Society Trustee and biographer of Quilliam)
Rumela Bandyopadhyay (New Beginnings)
Salih Whelbourne (Mu'allif Initiative)
Yahya Birt (community historian; Commemoration organiser)
Yusuf Chambers (City Retreat, Leicester)

*****

Participating Associations

Abdullah Quilliam Society
Cardiff New Muslims
City Retreat, Leicester
Convert Muslim Foundation
Fatima Elizabeth Phrontistery
Islamic Education and Research Academy (iERA)
Ihsan Mosque, Norwich
Leeds New Muslims
Liverpool Muslims
Luton Reverts Group
Mu'allif Initiative
New Beginnings
Solace UK
Welsh Muslim Cultural Foundation

Abbreviations

Endnotes

Chapter 1: A Fateful Meeting in Birkenhead

"Served as the association's secretary", Léon, 298; **"Half of Britain's shipping…"**, Geaves, 42; **"the most drunken…"**, *Times*, 28 Aug 1866, 8; **"The Temperance movement sought…"**, Schrad, 552–3; **"Some 40–50,000 seamen"**, Asmay, 20; **"Formerly known as the Temperance Child…"**, Geaves, 26–7; Winskill, 349; **"nine years as a defence lawyer"**, Seddon, 9; **"two Irish Fenian dynamitards"**, Abouhawas, "The Extraordinary Life"; Geaves, 31–2; **"Fanatics and Fanaticism"**, see Quilliam, *Fanatics*; also Byrne, 35; **"The Great Arabian teetotaler"**, *Manchester Examiner*, 10 Dec 1890, 8; **"the more hostile missionaries"**, Bennett, 119; **"an imposter and a blood-thirsty man"**, Cates, "How I Became", 142; **"I never knew that Muhammadans were teetotalers"**, Léon, 298; **"women do not have souls"**, Quilliam, "Half a Century"; **"Don't believe what I say…"**, Cates, "How I Became", 142.

Chapter 2: Frances' Humble Beginnings

"Yet he died…", John Murray [d. 13 May 1870], Death certificate, County of Chester, PRO (England), 14 May 1870; **"Alongside tuberculosis…"**, Robinson, 54; **"Agnes remarried…"**, Peter Cottam, Marriage Certificate, County of Lancaster, 15 Jun 1873; **"from tuberculosis to alcoholism…"**, Adams and Jordan, "Inflections".

Chapter 3: Rejection at Home

"Study it 'carefully'", Cates, "How I Became", 142; **"How dare you read…"**, Cates, ibid.; **"No, I will not…"**, Cates, ibid.; **"the most precious book…"**, Cates, ibid.; **"He answered Frances' question to him"**, Quilliam, *Faith*, 64; **"declared … [herself] a Moslem"**, Cates, "How I Became", 143.

Chapter 4: The First Call at Mount Vernon Hall

"Formed the Liverpool Muslim Society on 17 July 1887", Byrne, 35; Cates, "Liverpool Converts", 23; **"It was very hard work…"**, Cates, "How I Became", 143; **"was a constant attendant…"**, Léon, 298; **"a dilapidated state"**, *LM*, 1 Aug 1887, 7; **"that sat on the western side of Mount Vernon Street…"**, *Kelly's Directory*, 249; **"moral and social improvement"**, *LDP*, 30 Jul 1887, 6; *LM*, 1 Aug 1887, 7; **"first converts remained active in the Liverpool Temperance League…"**, *LM*, 1 Aug 1887, 7; *LM*, 18 Jan 1888, 6; *LM*, 27 Dec 1888, 6; **"We, the undersigned…"**, Cates, "Liverpool Converts", 23; **"for prayers and reading … the Koran"**, Léon, 298; **"non-sectarian"**, *LDP*, 30 Jul 1887, 6; *LM*, 1 Aug 1887, 7; **"Persons desirous of understanding MOSLEM THEOLOGY"**, *LM*, 31 May 1889, 3; **"Protestant Sunday Evensong…"**, Asmay, 10–13; **"the Sunday sermons that Quilliam gave … were elaborations of**

the letters he had written to Fatima", Léon, 298; Quilliam, *Faith*, 7; "frequently we got no audience but ourselves", *Manchester Examiner*, 10 Dec 1890, 8; "another convert was made…", Cates, "How I Became", 143; "For several months she was the only woman convert until…", Cates, "Liverpool Converts", 23; "It is impossible to describe…", Léon, 298; "would not have it occupied by any person…", Byrne, 35.

Chapter 5: Fatima's Leadership at Brougham Terrace

"Notice…", Monro, 5; Pool, 396; "a Christmas dinner for 230 poor children…", *LWC*, 28 Dec 1889, 6; "The muezzin would make the call to prayer…", Asmay, 75; "a nice little mosque…", Cates, "How I Became", 144; "the most intense period of violent persecution…", Singleton, 4–8; Geaves, 65–7; "Fatima acted as more than just the first Treasurer of England's first mosque community", Léon, 298; *TC*, 5 Aug 1893, 229; "represent the community externally…", BOA, Y. PRK. EŞA, 13/88, Ismail Lutfi Bey, Ottoman Trade Consul for Liverpool, investigative report on Liverpool Moslem Society [Liverpool Cemiyet-i Islamiyyesi], 25 Jun 1891; Abouhawas, "An Early Arab View"; "Fatima wrote to the *Liverpool Mercury*…", Cates, "The Marriage Question"; "the number of converts…", Byrne, 35; "Overall, a quarter of the converts were women …", Gilham, *Loyal Enemies*, 98–102; "the behaviour of the converts was 'nonsensical' (*behudgi*) and 'immodest' (*besharmi*)…", Monro, 16; "We try to observe the spirit of the Koran…", Monro, 26; "marrying him at the Anglican St. Peters Church", Marriage certificate of Hubert Henry Cates and Fatima Elizabeth Murray, Church of England, Parish of Liverpool, 28 Feb 1889; "My husband was then a Christian…", Cates, "How I Became", 144; "A younger sister of mine came…",

Cates, "How I Became", 144; **"Clara married one the young Indian students..."**, 1891 Census, 2 Marmaduke Street, Liverpool; *TC*, 1 Oct 1902, 217–18; **"how the work of proselytising..."**, Cates, "How I Became", 144; **"another one of her siblings ... also converted to Islam"**, Léon, 299; **"The flowers surrounding me..."**, *AR*, Vol. III, No. 7, Jul 1892, 80; **"Frederick, her only child, later had a career as an actor and playwright"**, R. Whittington-Egan, "Lonely last curtain for the Bowman of England", *Liverpool Echo*, 16 Feb 1972, 10; **"Hannah Rodda Robinson..."**, Winrow, 92–132; **"Gareth Winrow, Hannah's biographer, thinks..."**, Winrow, 114–15; **"there is nothing of devotion..."**, Monro, 41; **"Beset by numerous foes..."**; *A Collection of Hymns*, 40.

Chapter 6: Fatima and the Indian Muslims

"Wealthy, Anglicized Indian Muslims influenced by ... Sayyid Ahmad Khan", Saika and Raisur Rahman, 1–13, 89–107; **"the London Anjuman-i-Islam was established in 1886"**, Qureshi, 50; **"Moslem agent in England..."**, *The Homeward Mail*, 22 Jun 1889, 776, cited in Macnamara, "Abdullah Quilliam"; **"Ahmad gathered them together to formally make the declaration of faith"**, Monro, 31–2; **"the Mohammedan Anjuman of Liverpool"**, *The Civil and Military Gazette*, 25 Feb 1890, 8, cited in Macnamara, "Abdullah Quilliam"; **"Fatima also led on this promotional campaign..."**, *Glasgow Herald*, 1 Nov 1890, 7, cited in Macnamara, "Abdullah Quilliam"; **"You have no need to invite preachers..."**, Baksh, *Inglistan*, cited in Macnamara, "Abdullah Quilliam"; **"Ahmad published a letter..."**, *Times*, 26 Sep 1890, 4; **"Ahmad then wrote to Sultan Abdul Hamid II..."**, BOA, Y.PRK.ESA.00012.00028.001-3, cited in Macnamara, "Abdullah Quilliam"; Sharp, "On Behalf of the Sultan"; **"Ahmad, who left his position as Vice-President in 1891..."**, *The Bombay Gazette*, 6 Feb

1891, 6, cited in Macnamara, "Abdullah Quilliam"; **"Ahmad was able to get an introduction to the Ottoman caliph..."**, Ahmad, "Queen's Hindustani Diary"; Ahmad, "Sultan of Turkey"; Basu, 161–3; **"In 1890, the names of the officers of the Institute..."**, Anjuman Himayat-i-Islam (Lahore), *Risalah*, June 1890, 3–4, 12–13, cited in Pruss, 9 n.50; *AR*, Vol. I, No. 7, July 1890, 113–15; **"It was written in praise of the Begum of Bhopal..."**, Khan, *Begums of Bhopal*, 119–53; **"commissioned by G.W. Leitner (1840–99)..."**, Gilham, "Leitner".

Chapter 7: A Violent, Murderous Husband

"Four months after they were married ...", Divorce Court File: 14745; **"She had seen the shortcomings of the current divorce law..."**, Horstman, 20, 78; **"Rafiuddin Ahmad, whom she knew well and whose writings she had studied..."**, Ahmad, "Are English Women Legally Inferior".

Chapter 8: Travel to the East

"Fatima boarded the S.S. Anubis...", *Reis and Reyyet* (Calcutta), 10 Dec 1892, 567; **"the S.S. Anubis stopped at Gibraltar..."**, *Yarmouth Independent*, 15 Oct 1892, 4; **"returning in May 1893"**, *TC*, 13 May 1893, 132; **"She married another Muslim convert W.G. Ismail Winter..."**, Gilham, *Loyal Enemies*, 100; **"Fatima had travelled with Quilliam to Manchester..."**, Abouhawas, "An Early Arab View"; **"Amy met Ali Mokaiesh..."**, Macnamara, "From Arab Millet"; **"Fatima went on another trip to the South of England 'for a considerable period' in 1895"**, *TC*, 13 May 1896, 202; **"one large volume of photographs of scenery"**, *TC*, 6 Mar 1901, 153; **"The year 1894 was Fatima's last as Treasurer"**, *TC*, 5 Aug 1893, 229; *TC*, 12 Aug 1893, 239; Asmay, 127, 151.

Chapter 9: A Lonely Widow

"It is our melancholy duty...", "Up to the time of his death...", "Some ten days prior...", Léon, 298.

Chapter 10: A Moving Funeral

"Everything was simple...", Green, 299; "The chief mourners listed...", "The Sheikh was in attendance...", Green, 300; "O Fatima, say at the Gate of Heaven...", *Daily Dispatch* (Manchester), 1 Nov 1900, cited in *TC*, 7 Nov 1900, 301; "Oh, thou soul, which art at rest...", Quran 89: 27–8, Sale translation.

Chapter 11: The Secret Third Wife

"*The Crescent* records Cates' sudden death...", *TC*, 30 Jan 1895, 34; "Oh! silent hearts...", *TC*, 6 Feb 1895, 42; "'Tis so our sister yielded...", *TC*, 7 Nov 1900, 300–1; "could almost say of her as the Prophet said of Khadijah", *TC*, 24 Apr 1901, 260; "He was a fervent believer in polygamy...", Geaves, 57–8; "Hannah and Mary could not stand the sight of each other", Asmay, 92; "there were a lot of allegations in the mid-1890s about Quilliam's probity and character", Asmay, 16–25, 97–115; "a special meeting was held on 27 December 1896 by the London Anjuman-i-Islam", Anjuman-i-Islam, "Report"; "Fatima and Hubert Haleem ended up in West Kirby", *Gore's Directory*, 1058; "A Mother's Lullaby", Geaves and Birt, 40; "In 1907, Hubert's role as head of sixth form", *TC*, 3 Jul 1907, 12; "back from the front", *The Philomath*, Vol. 6, No. 265, Apr–Jun 1919, 61; "birth of Hubert's daughter", *The Philomath*, Vol. 8, No. 273, October 1921, 54; "Another big indication of Quilliam's fatherhood is that he named Hubert as an equal beneficiary...", PRO (England), Will of William Henry Quilliam of Liverpool, 23 Aug 1932.

Chapter 12: Fatima, Forgotten and Remembered

"Some communal memory of Quilliam and the Liverpool Muslims did persist...", Birt, "Preachers"; "Sariya Cheruvallil-Contractor, who points out...", Cheruvallil-Contractor, 69.

Bibliography

(*References reproduced in full in the Appendixes are listed in bold.*)

A Collection of Hymns Suitable for Use of the English Speaking Moslem Congregations (Liverpool: T. Dobb & Co., 1892).

Abouhawas, A., "An Early Arab View of Liverpool's Muslims", *Everyday Muslim*, 4 Mar 2020, https://www.everydaymuslim. org/blog/an-early-arab-view-of-liverpools-muslims/, accessed 26 Nov 2022.

Abouhawas, A., "The Extraordinary Life of Abdullah Quilliam: Part 1, 1856–1885", *Muslim Vibe*, 14 Sep 2019, https:// themuslimvibe.com/faith-islam/in-history/the-life-of-abdullah-quilliam-one-of-britains-most-famous-converts-to-islam, accessed 16 Nov 2022.

Adams, H.G., and C. Jordan, "Infections in the Alcoholic", *Medical Clinics of North America*, Vol. 68, 1984, 689–700.

Ahmad, R., "Are English Women Legally Inferior to Their Mamomedan Sisters?", *Asiatic Quarterly Review*, Vol. I, Jan–Apr 1891, 410–29.

Ahmad, R., "The Queen's Hindustani Diary", *The Strand Magazine* (London), Vol. IV, Jul–Sep 1892, 551–7.

Ahmad, R., "The Sultan of Turkey", *The Strand Magazine* (London), Vol. VI, Jul–Dec 1893, 571–82.

Anjuman-i-Islam London, "Report of Meeting 27 December 1896", Durham University Library, Pratt Green Collection, 263/1/329, 4pp.

Anon., "The Sheikh's Tribute to the Memory of the Deceased", *TC*, Vol. XVI, No. 408, 7 Nov 1900, 300-1.

Asmay, Y.S., *Islam in Victorian Liverpool: An Ottoman Account of Britain's First Mosque Community*, trans. and ed. by Y. Birt, R. Macnamara and M.Z. Maksudoğlu (Swansea: Claritas Books, 2021).

Bakhsh, K., *Inglistan mein Islam* [Islam in England] (Lahore, 1891).

Basu, S., *Victoria & Abdul* (Stroud: The History Press, 2011).

Bennett, C., "Victorian Images of Islam", *International Bulletin of Missionary Research*, Vol. 15, No. 3, 1991, 115-19.

Birt, Y., "Preachers, Patriots and Islamists: Contemporary British Muslims and the Afterlives of Abdullah Quilliam" in J. Gilham and R. Geaves (eds.), *Victorian Muslim: Abdullah Quilliam and Islam in the West* (London: Hurst, 2017), 133-150, 201-5.

Byrne, O., "A Short History of the Progress of Islam in England", *TC*, Vol. XI, No. 262, 19 Jan 1898, 35-6.

Cates, F.E., "A Moslimah's Prayer", *AR*, Vol. III, No. 9, Sep 1892, 144.

Cates, F.E., "How I Became a Muhammadan", *AR*, Vol. II, No. X, Oct 1891, 142-4.

Cates, F.E., "Khadija", *TC*, Vol. II, No. 36, 23 Sep 1893, 288.

Cates, F.E., "On the Folly of Heeding Scandal", *TC*, Vol. XVI, No. 409, 14 Nov 1900 [1890], 307-10.

Cates, F.E., "The Liverpool Converts: Correct Details", *AR*, Vol. III, No. 2, Feb 1892, 22–4.

Cates, F.E., "The Marriage Question", *LM*, 16 Apr 1891, 6; 17 Apr 1891, 5.

Cheruvallil-Contractor, S., "Women in Britain's First Mosques: Hidden from History, but Not Without Influence" in S. Gilliat-Ray and R. Timol (eds.), *Leadership, Authority and Representation in British Muslim Communities* (Basel: MDPI, 2020), 61–72.

Geaves, R., *Islam in Victorian Britain: The Life and Times of Abdullah Quilliam* (Markfield, Leicestershire: Kube Publishing, 2010).

Geaves, R. and Y. Birt (eds.) *The Collected Poems of Abdullah Quilliam* (Oldham: Beacon Books, 2021).

Gilham, J., "Professor G. W. Leitner in England: The Oriental Institute, Woking Mosque, Islam and Relations with Muslims, 1884–1899", *Islam and Christian–Muslim Relations*, 2020, DOI: 10.1080/09596410.2020.1851932.

Gilham, J., *Loyal Enemies: British Converts to Islam, 1850–1950* (London: Hurst, 2014).

Gore's Directory of Liverpool and Birkenhead, Part 2 (London: Kelly's Directories, 1900)

Green, G.H., "The Funeral", *TC*, Vol. XVI, No. 408, 7 Nov 1900, 299–300.

Horstman, A., *Victorian Divorce* (New York: St. Martin's Press, 1985).

Kelly's Directory of Liverpool and Suburbs (London: Kelly & Co., 1894), Part I.

Khan, S.M., *The Begums of Bhopal: A Dynasty of Women Rulers in Raj India* (London: I.B. Tauris, 2000).

Khattak, S.K.K., *Islam and the Victorians: Nineteenth Century Perceptions of Muslim Practices* and Beliefs (London: I.B. Tauris, 2008).

Léon, H.M., "Death of Sister Fatima Cates", *TC*, Vol. 16, No. 408, 1900, 298–9.

Macnamara, R., "Abdullah Quilliam and the Indian Muslims: The Making of a Muslim Mission in Liverpool (1889–96)", forthcoming.

Macnamara, R., "From Arab Millet to British Islam: Syrian Muslims in Victorian Manchester", forthcoming.

Monro, J., *Moslems in Liverpool, a series of papers contributed by Dr. Henry Martyn Clark, C.M.S. to the Punjab Mission News* [1891] (Calcutta: Joseph Culshaw, 1901).

Pool, J.J., *Mohammedanism, Historical and Doctrinal, with a chapter on Islam in England* (London: Archibald Constable, 1892).

Pruss, M.-M., "The 'Church of Islam': esotericism, Orientalism, and religious origin myths in colonial South Asia", *Journal of the Royal Asiatic Society*, Series 3, 2022, 1–24.

Quilliam, W.H., *Fanatics and Fanaticism: A Lecture* (Liverpool: T. Dobb & Co., 1890), 2nd edition.

Quilliam, W.H., *The Faith of Islam: An Explanatory Sketch of the Principal Fundamental Tenets of the Moslem Religion* (Liverpool: Wilmer Brother & Co., 1892), 3rd edition.

Quilliam, W.H.A., ""Half a Century of Islam in England: An Early English Muslim Speaks" [translation], *Al-Fath*, No. 108, 1928, 113–16, http://www.abdullahquilliam.org/cairo-speech-1928/, accessed 16 Nov 2022.

Qureshi, M.N., *Pan-Islam in British Indian Politics: A Study of the Khilafat Movement, 1918–1924* (Leiden: Brill, 1999).

Robinson, A., *Imagining London, 1770–1900* (Basingstoke, Hampshire: Palgrave MacMillan, 2004).

Saika, Y. and M. Raisur Rahman (eds.), *The Cambridge Companion to Sayyid Ahmad Khan* (Cambridge: University Press, 2019).

Schrad, M.K., *Smashing the Liquor Machine: A Global History of Prohibition* (New York: Oxford University Press, 2021).

Seddon, M.S., "Abdullah Quilliam: A Muslim Revolutionary Socialist", in J. Gilham and R. Geaves (eds.), *Victorian Muslim: Abdullah Quilliam and Islam in the West* (London: Hurst, 2017), 7–23.

Sharp, M.A., "On Behalf of the Sultan: The Late Ottoman State and the Cultivation of British and American Converts to Islam", Ph.D. thesis, University of Pennsylvania, Near Eastern Languages and Civilizations, 2020.

Singleton, B., "'Heave Half a Brick at Him': Hate Crimes and Discrimination against Muslim Converts in Late Victorian Liverpool", *Journal of Muslim Minority Affairs*, Vol. 37, No. 1, 1–13, 2017, DOI: 10.1080/13602004.2017.1294376.

TNA, Public Records, Divorce Court File: 14745, Appellant: Francess Elizabeth Cates. Respondent: Hubert Henry Cates.

Winrow, G., *Whispers Across Continents: In Search of the Robinsons* (Stroud, Gloucestershire, UK: Amberley, 2019).

Winskill, P.T., *Temperance Standard Bearers of the Nineteenth Century: A Biographical and Statistical Temperance Dictionary* (Manchester: Darrah Bros, 1898).

Acknowledgements

Yahya Birt would like to thank Hamid Mahmood first of all for generously giving him the opportunity to work with him as the leading researcher into the life of Fatima Elizabeth Cates. It has been Hamid's hard work over the last decade into the primary sources that has shed new light on Fatima's life. He would also like to thank Riordan Macnamara for kindly sharing his unpublished research on the relationships that the Syrian traders of Manchester and the Indian Muslims of London had with the Liverpool Muslim Institute. Last but not least, Yahya thanks Fozia, Sulayman, and Layla for their amazing and loving support.

Hamid Mahmood would like to thank Yahya Birt for his endless endeavour in researching the history of Islam in Britain and more specifically working on this manuscript to provide a wider context to the life of Fatima Elizabeth Cates. He would also like to thank Abdurahman Abouhawas, for sharing his research on Quilliam and Fatima Cates over the years and providing a critical eye over the primary sources. Also, he would like to thank Daood Dhami, Maryam Sadak and Talha Samin for working on the primary source transcriptions, and Aquifa Razzaq and Zanib Yaqoob for providing valuable feedback. The love and interest in the story of Fatima shown by his wonderful students at Mill Hill County High School never went unnoticed. Lastly, he would like to send his heartfelt appreciation to all the staff, students and parents at Fatima Elizabeth Phrontistery for their unwavering interest in the life of Fatima Elizabeth Cates, and prayers for his late parents, Ismail Abid and Rashida Begum.

We are both indebted to Sariya Cheruvallil-Contractor, Ron Geaves, Christina Longden, and Riordan Macnamara for kindly reading and commenting upon a draft of this manuscript. We would also like to thank Jamil Chishti and the team at Beacon Books for giving us the opportunity to publish with them, and for turning this book around so quickly in time for the Fatima Elizabeth Cates Commemoration on 21 January 2023 in Liverpool at the Abdullah Quilliam Mosque.

There is no success or triumph except in God's acceptance, so may this book be a means for good in this world and the next by God's mercy, amin.

Author Biodata

Yahya Birt is a community historian who has taught at the University of Leeds, has published over a dozen peer-reviewed articles on Islam in Britain and co-edited *British Secularism and Religion* (2016), *Islam in Victorian Liverpool* (2021) and most recently, *The Collected Poems of Abdullah Quilliam* (2021). He is a founding series editor for the Oxford British Muslim Studies series published by the Oxford University Press. In 2022, he published his first poetry collection, *Pandemic Pilgrimage*, reflecting on performing Umrah under Covid. He is Research Director at the London-based think-tank, the Ayaan Institute, where he works on Muslim minorities. His first report was released in 2022 called *Ummah at the Margins: The Past, Present, and Future of Muslim Minorities*. He lives in West Yorkshire with his family and cat. He likes walking and being grumpy about the state of the world. He can be reached on Twitter @ybirt.

Hamid Mahmood is the founder of Fatima Elizabeth Phrontistery, an Islamic supplementary school (*madrasa*) based in London. He studied traditional *'alimiyya* at the seminary, the

Institute of Islamic Education in Dewsbury, West Yorkshire. He continued his secular education at Heythrop College and Queen Mary, University of London, where he completed his Masters' thesis on *The Dars-e-Nizami and the Transnational Traditionalist Madaris in Britain* (2012). He is interested in the history of Islam and the West, and his recent focus has been on Islam in Victorian England in particular the life of Fatima Elizabeth Cates. He named his *madrasa* after Fatima Elizabeth in order to bring her story to life, and Prophetic consciousness in educational pedagogy is at the heart of the phrontistery's philosophy. He likes cycling and archery, and has founded the Fatima Elizabeth Archery Club, where he coaches on the fusion of Eastern and Western archery. He is a teacher by profession and lives in London with his wife Tayyaba, and three daughters, Juwairiyyah, Barakah and Halimah. He can be reached on info@fatimaelizabethphrontistery.co.uk

ALSO AVAILABLE FROM BEACON BOOKS

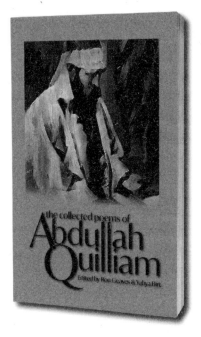

The Collected Poems of Abdullah Quilliam brings together the secular and religious poetry of Abdullah Quilliam (1856–1932) in a single volume for the first time.

Best known as the founder of Britain's first mosque community, this collection covers his entire four-decade poetic output, and reveals much about his inner spiritual and emotional life, about the private man behind the public figure.

Read more, **be** more.
www.beaconbooks.net

ALSO AVAILABLE FROM BEACON BOOKS

Marmaduke Pickthall: British Muslim is a biography of Marmaduke William Pickthall – a convert to Islam and one of the most renowned translators of the Qur'an. But Pickthall was much more than an historical oddity or gifted translator: he was a novelist, journalist, political and religious leader, and an often confusing mix of allegiances and beliefs.

Oriental Encounters is the best introduction to Pickthall's work, a fictionalised account of his experiences, including tales he heard during his travels in Syria. Full of freshness and high spirits, it details his first encounters with the Middle East, his alienation from his fellow-Englishmen and his affection for the people of Syria and Palestine.

Read more, *be* more.
www.beaconbooks.net